150 TIPS AND TRICKS

for New Dads

From the First Feeding to Diaper-Changing Disasters—
Everything You Need to Know to Be a Great Father

Vincent Iannelli, MD

Avon, Massachusetts

Published by
Adams Media, a division of F+W Media, Inc.
57 Littlefield Street, Avon, MA 02322. U.S.A.
www.adamsmedia.com

Contains material adapted and abridged from *The Everything® Father's First
Year Book*, by Vincent Iannelli, MD, copyright © 2005 by F+W Media, Inc.,
ISBN 10: 1-59337-310-4, ISBN 13: 978-1-59337-310-8.

ISBN 10: 1-60550-347-9
ISBN 13: 978-1-60550-347-9

Printed in the United States of America.

J I H G F E D C B A

Library of Congress Cataloging-in-Publication Data
is available from the publisher.

This publication is designed to provide accurate and authoritative information
with regard to the subject matter covered. It is sold with the understanding that
the publisher is not engaged in rendering legal, accounting, or other professional
advice. If legal advice or other expert assistance is required, the services of a
competent professional person should be sought.

—From a *Declaration of Principles* jointly adopted by a Committee of the
American Bar Association and a Committee of Publishers and Associations

Many of the designations used by manufacturers and sellers to distinguish their
product are claimed as trademarks. Where those designations appear in this
book and Adams Media was aware of a trademark claim, the designations have
been printed with initial capital letters.

This book is available at quantity discounts for bulk purchases.
For information, please call 1-800-289-0963.

Contents

Introduction
Becoming a Dad

You've heard it before: Having a baby changes everything. And it's true. From the way you keep your home to the way you spend your spare time, life as you know it is about to change forever. As an expecting dad, you're probably feeling all kinds of different emotions, from anxiety to excitement. Hopefully you've begun to think about what kind of dad you want to be. Your past experiences with your own father and other role models, as well as your personal feelings about fatherhood, will undoubtedly affect the way you act as a father.

Take a moment and think about it—What does being a good father mean to you? It's going to mean different things for different families, but there are a few key things to remember. Being a dad isn't really about how much money you make, all of the things you can buy your family, or how successful you are at work. It's more about being available and supporting your family with your love and attention. Being an equal partner when it comes to taking care of your baby is another one of the most important qualities of a good father. Your baby's mother is going to need a lot of help and support from you, and your ability to work together as a team will make you a strong support system for your baby.

Here's one simple piece of advice that will help you throughout your years as a father—Ask for help when you need it. Dads are often reluctant to admit that they're feeling confused, worried, or lost in a given situation. But once you become a father, your responsibility is to your child. That means swallowing your pride and doing whatever it takes to get the information and support you need to be a good parent. You'll find that there are countless resources out there to help you, and that other parents who were once in your shoes will be happy to share their wisdom with you.

If you're still feeling nervous about the challenges that lie ahead or fearful that you won't be able to fulfill all your fatherly duties, don't worry. You're right on schedule, and you're in good company. This book contains all the tips and tricks you need to help you find answers to your toughest questions, get support and reassurance when you need it, and navigate those first few weeks and months when you're still figuring things out. And that will leave more time for what's really important—your relationship with your new baby!

Part One

Pre-Baby Preparation

An expecting dad has a lot of work to do to prepare for the baby. In addition to tangible tasks such as stocking up on supplies, choosing a crib and bedding, and designing the nursery, a dad-to-be also needs to make emotional preparations for all the lifestyle changes to come. This is also a good time to think about important medical topics, such as cord blood banking, newborn screening, and whether or not to circumcise your baby boy.

Prepare for Big Changes

First-time dads who think that their lives won't change much are in for a very big surprise. You probably enjoy a lot of luxuries and freedoms now that you take for granted. When you become a father, you won't be able to go out each night, watch every sporting event on TV, or spend all of your free time playing golf. You will need to use a lot more of what used to be free time taking care of your baby.

Other changes you can expect when you have a new baby can include:

- Needing to be more flexible with your time
- Being less spontaneous
- Getting by with less sleep
- Having less time alone with your partner

This may not sound like much fun, but remember, there are plenty of positives to having a child, too! Chief among them is having the unconditional love of your baby. Becoming a parent is one of the most reward-ing experiences life has to offer, and while it does have its challenges, remember that having a baby is not all about the things that you are going to give up or have less time for. It just makes things easier in the long run if you go into this new time of your life with a good idea of what to expect.

Just because you should be more available to help at home and with your baby doesn't mean that you can't still make time for other things that are important to you. As with other busy times in your life, you just have to set your priorities and give up some of the less important things you used to spend time doing. Take a good look at your usual schedule and see which things show up more often than they should. Do you really need to go for a drink after work with the guys, spend several hours on the Internet, or watch whatever is on TV at night?

Not everything you do is going to be equally important, so learn to set priorities to better manage your time. Your priorities still can (and should) include some time for yourself. This means that in addition to your new role as the helpful father, you can probably still play your usual rounds of golf if, for example, you give up watching sports on TV in the evening. Or if you like working out at a health club regularly, switch your workouts to the early morning so that you can head home right after work to take over caring for your baby. As long as your top priority is your family, you should be able to balance the rest of your time to fit in the other activities that are important to you.

Part One: Pre-Baby Preparation

3 | Learn What Is Expected of You

Knowing what role to take that first month after his baby is born can be difficult for a new dad. The role of the new mom is well defined, but dads don't always know what's expected of them. And different families will have different needs and expectations, which can make things even more confusing. Sometimes, even when parents-to-be agree on the roles they each will take, their expectations and needs change once the baby comes home. When this happens, parents often can just re-evaluate their roles and try to change the way that they are doing things.

When you're trying to determine your role, it can help to simply have a talk with the new mom to figure out what your family needs from you. Should you try to stay home from work for a few weeks? Should you help care for the baby—for example, taking over some feedings and changing diapers—or should you just help around the house?

If Mom wants to spend most of her time bonding with her baby, having Dad take over some extra household chores can be extremely helpful. So you might do the laundry, cook the meals, or buy groceries, if those aren't things that you already are doing. For a new mom who just needs to catch up on sleep, it could be most helpful to take over with the baby for a while and give Mom a break.

Choosing a name for your new baby can be one of the most fun things you do before your baby is born. Enjoy this opportunity to dream and tell stories with your partner. Flip through baby name books together. Visit baby name websites. Discuss the names you each had in mind for your future baby when you were growing up. Do you still like those names today? How does your partner like the names you have in mind? What does each of you think a name means to an individual? While all of this baby name talk will be enjoyable, you still have a task at hand: to choose one name for your baby.

The baby's middle name might simply include a name that you like, or it could be the name of a friend or family member whom you want to honor. Be sure to check the initials so your child doesn't end up with a monogram such as FAT or PIG.

Sticking to a family tradition for naming your baby can be a good way to honor or remember your ancestors, but whose tradition do you follow? What if both Mom's and Dad's families have a tradition of naming the first-born child after their own grandparents?

In this kind of situation, if you can't reach a compromise, you might come up with your own "tradition." Maybe name all of your children with names that start with a certain letter. Or name your first girl after the mom's mother and your first boy after the dad's father.

Get a Car Seat

Shopping for a car seat, with so many different brands and types available, can be overwhelming. You need to follow different basic guidelines depending on the car you drive and the type of seat you're looking for. As the American Academy of Pediatrics states, there is no "safest" or "best" car seat, so in the end your choice will come down to personal preference.

Infant-Only Carriers

Your first car seat will probably be an infant-only seat. This seat is designed for young infants and the rear-facing position that is safest for them. (The American Academy of Pediatrics and the National Highway Traffic Safety Administration both urge parents to have their babies ride rear-facing until they are *both* one year old and weigh twenty pounds.) One of the best features of an infant-only seat is that after installing a detachable base into the backseat of your car, you can just snap the seat into the base when you are ready to go. When you reach your destination, detach the seat and use it as a carrier to transport your baby.

Most infant seats can only be used for babies who weigh less than twenty pounds. If you use an infant seat and your baby reaches twenty pounds before his first birthday, then you will have to get a convertible seat and use it in the rear-facing position for a while.

Convertible Car Seats

This type of seat is "convertible" because it can be used in both the rear-facing and forward-facing positions, accommodating newborns, infants, and most toddlers. These seats can be used until a child weighs about forty pounds. Some convertible car seats with higher weight limits can be used as a belt-positioning booster seat for children up to sixty-five or even eighty pounds. While this means that you might be able to use just one car seat until your child is three years old (and therefore buy only one), a convertible seat might not fit your newborn well, and it can't be used as a carrier.

Learn How to Position a Car Seat

Car seats have always been hard to use, and most experts estimate that 85 percent of parents use them incorrectly. Be sure to read the manufacturer's instructions so that you install and use your car seat correctly. LATCH (Lower Anchors and Tethers for Children) is a system that is installed in newer cars and car seats to make them much easier to install.

Although it sometimes depends on how many other kids you have seated in the car and where the seat fits best, in almost all cases your baby will be safest in the middle of the backseat. In addition to keeping your baby away from side-impact collisions, it protects him from any danger from side air bags. Whichever seat you choose, remember to place your baby in the rear-facing position until he weighs twenty pounds and is twelve months old.

Rear-facing car seats cannot be used in a seat with an air bag. Because your younger child must be seated rear-facing in the car, you will have to make other arrangements if your car or truck doesn't have a backseat.

One alternative is to turn off your passenger-side air bag when you have your baby in the car. The National Highway Traffic Safety Administration (NHTSA) has a form that you can use to request an air bag on-off switch if you have an infant who must ride in the front seat.

These days everyone knows that smoking cigarettes is a very unhealthy habit, resulting in such deadly conditions as lung cancer; however, that doesn't stop some people from continuing to smoke. The decision to smoke or not is a personal choice, but people considering becoming parents should be aware of the extremely negative effects that secondhand smoke can have on babies and children. One of the healthiest things that you can do, for your baby and yourself, is make your home smoke-free. If you smoke, the best time to quit is now, before your baby is born and you bring him home.

Lower the Temperature of Your Water

Younger children, especially newborns, have very sensitive skin that can burn easily. They also usually are not able to quickly pull away from burning water or let you know if the water is too hot, so it is important to protect your child from hot water to prevent scalding burns.

Simply testing the water is not enough, because your infant may turn the water faucet on herself and quickly get burned if the water temperature is too hot. The best precaution to take is to turn down the temperature of your hot water heater now, before you even bring the baby home.

To give you a better idea of how sensitive your baby's skin is, this is how quickly she can get a third-degree burn:

- In only two seconds if the water temperature is 150°F
- In only five seconds if the water temperature is 140°F
- In thirty seconds if the water temperature is 130°F
- In about five minutes if the water temperature is 120°F

Could you get your baby away from the water in two or even five seconds if she is playing with the hot water tap and manages to turn it on? Probably not, and that's all the reason you need to lower your hot water heater temperature to no hotter than 120°F. It's not always easy to see exactly what temperature a water heater is set at, so even after lowering your heater's temperature, it is a good idea to test the water with a cooking thermometer. (Run the water until it's as hot as it gets, fill a mug with the hot water, and check its temperature.)

Also be sure to test the water before you use it near your baby each time, especially if you are lowering her into a bath, and never leave your kids unsupervised in the bathroom or kitchen.

Consider Cord Blood Banking

Storing your baby's umbilical cord stem cells in a cord blood bank has the potential to save her if she some-day gets seriously sick. Once collected, stored, and saved, umbilical cord stem cells can later be used for a stem cell transplant if your child develops a genetic dis-ease or a type of blood disorder or cancer that can be treated with a bone marrow transplant. Because your baby's cord blood must be collected at the time she is born, you will have to think about and be prepared to have her cord blood collected while you are still expect-ing. This is not a decision you can make later.

The marketing of the cord blood banks that describe a "once-in-a-lifetime opportunity" can be persuasive, but the procedure is expensive. After a one-time bank-ing fee of about $1,500 to $1,700, you will have to pay about $95 a year to store the stem cells. Even with payment plans, that is a lot of money for most new parents.

It doesn't hurt your baby to take the blood from the cut umbilical cord, and this blood would just be thrown out if you decided not to save it. That seems to leave money as the main deciding factor. If it is something that you can afford and you feel better knowing that you are storing your baby's stem cells in case you ever need them, then signing up with a cord blood bank might be for you.

When making your decision, keep in mind the clinical report on cord blood banking by the American Academy of Pediatrics (AAP) concluded that "private storage of cord blood as 'biological insurance' is unwise." In other words, the AAP doesn't think that it is necessary for the average parent to store their child's cord blood. However, it may be a good idea if you already have a family member who needs or may need a stem cell transplant because they have leukemia, a severe hemoglobinopathy, or other disorder, both because they may be able to use your baby's cord blood for a transplant and because your child may be at increased risk of developing these conditions too. The AAP does recommend that parents donate their babies' stem cells to nonprofit centers, such as the National Marrow Donor Program cord blood banks, so that they can be used for stem cell transplants in unrelated recipients.

Consider Newborn Screening Tests

Not all birth defects can be easily recognized at birth, because many don't cause symptoms until weeks or even years later. However, some birth defects can be found through newborn screening tests. Many of the illnesses that are screened for can cause severe mental retardation or even death.

Among the disorders that can be easily screened for are the following:

- Phenylketonuria (PKU)
- Galactosemia
- Congenital hypothyroidism
- Sickle-cell disease
- Congenital adrenal hyperplasia (CAH)
- Homocystinuria
- Maple syrup urine disease (MSUD)
- Cystic fibrosis
- Medium chain Acyl-CoA Dehydrogenase (MCAD) deficiency
- Glucose-6-Phosphate Dehydrogenase (G6PD) deficiency

Most of these disorders cannot be totally cured, but they can be easily treated. There are medications for congenital hypothyroidism and CAH, and special diets for PKU, galactosemia, and MSUD. Depending on where you live, your baby may only be screened for PKU and congenital hypothyroidism, or he may be screened for all of these conditions and more. Your pediatrician or state health department can let you know what your baby will be automatically screened for.

For parents who want more extensive screening, expanded or supplemental screening tests are also available. The blood specimen for these tests can be taken at the same time that the state screen is done. It's possible to test for an additional thirty to fifty diseases from a single specimen of blood. Although each disease that is screened for is rare, the tests are relatively inexpensive, costing about $25 to $60 for all of them, and so can be a good idea for parents who want some additional reassurance. Start thinking now about whether you want to pay for extra tests or check with your insurance company to see if this is a covered benefit.

Make a Decision about Circumcision

Even though getting a baby boy circumcised can be a controversial topic, parents usually have a strong opinion one way or the other about whether or not a circumcision is a necessary procedure. Circumcision is another thing you and your partner need to think about and discuss before your baby is born, so that you don't feel rushed into making a decision.

If you are considering circumcising your baby boy, keep in mind the new American Academy of Pediatrics (AAP) Circumcision Policy Statement, which states that "data are not sufficient to recommend routine neonatal circumcision." So why would anyone circumcise their baby if the AAP doesn't recommend it? One big reason is that although the AAP doesn't formally recommend that babies be circumcised, they don't actually recommend against it, either. Instead they conclude that "parents should determine what is in the best interest of the child," which leaves open many reasons for why a baby might be circumcised, including religious or cultural reasons, or just because Dad or an older sibling is already circumcised.

Still, there are many reasons why you may not want to circumcise your baby. One of the biggest is that although it is a minor procedure, it is still a surgical procedure. And like most medical or surgical procedures, there can be risks, including excessive bleeding and infections. Other risks or complications can include your doctor taking off too much skin or too little skin, so that the circumcision has to be repeated at some later time. Even though these side effects are uncommon, if you add in the fact that the benefits are also small, such as the small decrease in the rate of urinary tract infections, choosing to not have your baby circumcised is a valid decision.

If your child is going to be circumcised, you should insist that the doctor use some type of analgesia to try to decrease the pain your baby may feel. This might include a topical anesthetic, such as EMLA Cream, or an injection of lidocaine in a penile nerve block. The days of believing that babies don't feel pain are long over.

12   Make a Will

Younger couples often overlook the need to have a will. After all, they don't expect anything to happen to them anytime soon, and they probably haven't built up many assets yet. Once a baby is born, however, a will becomes absolutely essential.

Without a will, if both you and your baby's mother die, you will have no control over who becomes your baby's guardian. Do you want family members to fight over your baby, have a court pick someone, or have your baby go to a foster home? Or would you rather put some thought into who would best raise your baby and make sure that they have the legal right to do so? Whatever you do, don't put off creating a will. If you wait too long, you might forget, and then it could be too late.

For most new parents, unless they already have a lot of money or financial assets, the cost of preparing a will shouldn't be a big issue. A basic will that is easy to prepare is likely to be all you need, and you may not even need a lawyer to do it. A wide choice of software and self-help books are available to help you prepare a simple will on your own, inexpensively. However, you should hire a lawyer if you need more than just a basic will. In complicated situations—for example, if you are not married to your baby's mother, have children from a previous marriage, or already have a lot of financial assets—a lawyer should help you prepare your will.

Double (or Triple) the Preparations if You're Expecting Multiples

In general, parents have about a 3 percent chance of having twins or other multiples, such as triplets or quadruplets. For older couples or those who used fertility treatments, the chances are even higher. While your chance of having twins is increased if there are fraternal twins in your family, there is no increased chance if other family members only have identical twins. Identical twins are thought to occur randomly and are not tied to genetics.

Although each bundle of joy is definitely a blessing, if you are going to have more than one at once, there is a lot more preparation to do. Having multiples means buying more of everything as you prepare for your babies. You will need more clothing, more diapers, and more of just about everything else. You will need more than one car seat and eventually, more than one crib. Of course that means having to spend more money than you would if you only had one baby at a time, and it also means that you are likely to need more help caring for them. This is a situation in which a father might try to take more paternity leave or ask another family member to come help with the babies. Fathers of multiples should also expect to help out a lot more than what they might have expected for only one baby.

14   Consider the Details if You're Adopting

A lot of preparation goes into the whole adoption process, starting with signing up with an adoption agency and going all the way to the day that you actually get to take your child home. There is the paperwork, waiting, and all of the regular preparations to get your home ready for a baby. Also consider the costs that can be associated with adopting, depending on your adopted child's situation and location. If you plan on adopting, it's a very good idea to put extra money aside for such expenses.

If you are adopting a child from another country, there may also be medical issues to prepare for. Does the child have any special health-care needs? Does he need immunizations or screening tests to detect common infectious diseases, such as HIV, tuberculosis, and hepatitis? Your pediatrician can help you review your adopted child's health once you adopt your baby.

Be Extra Prepared if You Have Children with Special Needs

Infants with special needs can be much harder to understand than the average baby. They may need to feed more frequently or more slowly, require special medical attention, or have other things you need to do to help them feed and grow. Of course, these babies really are special, and you will love and care for yours just as you would any other baby.

Whether you have a premature baby who is a little behind in everything, or a child with Down syndrome or a cleft lip and palate, you will have to learn to understand your baby's own special needs. Your pediatrician, a specialist or other health professional, or a support group can help you learn how to best take care of your baby with special needs.

In most cases of children with special needs, extra financial planning is necessary. Your child may need medical treatments or surgical procedures, alternative schooling or therapy, or any number of other special arrangements and considerations. Putting money aside as early as possible for such events is always a wise move. The good news is that depending on your child's special needs, there may be other sources of help and support available to you in the form of national organizations, charities, and other support groups. These groups might be able to offer financial support, information, and comfort in your difficult times.

Part Two

The First Hours, Days, and Weeks

Get ready, because here is where it all starts. Once your baby arrives, it will soon hit you that you're a new dad. Although the first few days can be overwhelming, they are also fun and exciting. This is a time that you will always remember. Knowing what to expect and what is going on with your baby can help make these days even more enjoyable.

Know Your Role During the Birth

Once your baby is born, a lot of different things can happen in the delivery room. Although it is now routine for fathers to be in the labor and delivery room with the mother when their babies are being born, it can sometimes be hard for an expecting dad to know his place. You probably will be feeling anxious, confused, nervous, excited, or some combination of all of these feelings. Remember that your primary role is going to be to coach and comfort the expecting mother. If you don't know what to do beyond this, just ask someone. No matter how many books you read or classes you take, this experience is not something that you can easily prepare for. However, the more relaxed and calm you are when the big moment arrives, the more you'll be able to support Mom during labor.

Usually the first thing that will happen once the baby is born is that the cord will be cut. Then, if it was an uncomplicated vaginal delivery, the mother might be given a few moments with the baby. If it was a caesarean section or if the baby is limp or blue, he might immediately be taken away to be resuscitated.

This procedure is best suited for a newborn that comes out and is not breathing or doesn't have a heartbeat; however, even crying, healthy newborns often undergo the same basic initial resuscitation procedure. After delivery, a baby who needs resuscitation is handed off to someone from the resuscitation team—a nurse, pediatrician, or some other health professional—who takes him over to an infant warmer. There the baby will be dried off, positioned on the warmer, and have his nose and mouth suctioned. The baby will then have his breathing or heart rate stimulated if necessary, although a crying newborn who is breathing well will likely not need this additional stimulation.

Once on the warmer, the baby will be quickly dried off to prevent heat loss, especially if he seems sick. Next, the baby is positioned so that his airway can be seen, and then his mouth is suctioned to get any leftover fluid out. After these procedures, if the baby still isn't breathing well on his own, the health professional will stimulate him to breathe by slapping his foot or firmly rubbing his back. The baby is likely to respond to this extra stimulation and start breathing and crying well on his own.

Keep in mind that not all babies cry a lot after they are born. Parents often listen for the sound of loud crying to signal that their baby is healthy. If your baby stops crying after a few cries but is awake and alert, pink and breathing well, then she is likely to be healthy and doing fine.

After the resuscitation, your baby will be wrapped in a blanket and handed back to either Mom or Dad. You may not be thinking about feeding your baby at this time, but if your baby's mother plans on breastfeeding, now would be a good time to start if she is feeling up to it. This is especially important, because after being awake and alert for an hour or two, your baby is likely to sleep most of the rest of his first day and will be harder to wake up for breastfeeding. Additionally, while you're still at the hospital, there will be staff available, such as nurses or lactation counselors, to help you and Mom with any initial breastfeeding issues. Once you go home, you'll be on your own. Even if Mom isn't breastfeeding, you both should spend the first hour after delivery holding and bonding with your new baby if he is healthy and doesn't have to be taken immediately to the nursery.

Part Two: The First Hours, Days, and Weeks

Prepare for the Possibility of Premature Birth or Sickness

Although it's common to hear of full-term babies being born at 38 to 42 weeks, only babies born before 35 weeks are usually considered to be premature. Older preterm babies, like those born between 35 and 37 weeks, usually do just as well as those born full-term.

Your premature baby will likely need to spend some time in a neonatal intensive care unit (NICU). How long mostly depends on how early your baby was and what complications she has. A good rule of thumb is that your baby probably will be discharged from the NICU close to her expected due date. If your baby is a preemie or gets sick shortly after being born and his mother is still recovering herself, a good job for Dad is to gather information about what is going on with his baby. Doctors should be able to give quick, regular updates.

Being "sick" typically means that your baby is having difficulty breathing or is showing some other signs of an infection. Standard procedures in situations like this usually involve your pediatrician examining your baby, ordering a blood count and blood cultures to look for an infection, and starting intravenous fluids and antibiotics for a few days. If all testing is normal and your child quickly recovers, the antibiotics are often stopped after forty-eight hours. Other testing might include a chest x-ray to look for pneumonia or other lung problems, and blood sugar monitoring.

If your baby is just a few weeks early or isn't very sick, she might be able to stay in a regular nursery. Sicker babies or preemies born before 35 weeks will likely need to be transferred to a neonatal intensive care unit or NICU. If there is a NICU in the hospital where your baby was born, the transfer will be easy, but it is possible that the baby will have to be transferred to a larger hospital with more advanced facilities.

A transfer can be especially hard because the mother won't be able to see her baby until she is discharged herself. She should be able to see her baby briefly before the transfer, though, and will get frequent updates over the phone or from you after you visit the NICU.

Know What Happens in the Nursery

Whether your baby is sick or well, he will eventually be taken to the nursery. Once there, he will be weighed, measured, and observed to make sure that no problems develop. Other routine procedures will include:

- A sponge bath
- A vitamin K shot
- Eye drops or ointment to prevent infection
- Observation to make sure he can maintain a normal body temperature
- Observation for difficulty breathing, heart murmurs, and color changes
- A first feeding of sugar water if your baby's mother isn't breastfeeding

At-risk babies might also have blood sugar testing if they are very small or very large. Babies whose mothers had a positive Group B Strep test might have additional testing and antibiotics for a few days.

Once it has been determined that your baby is healthy, and his temperature doesn't drop when he isn't under a warmer, he probably will be able to leave the nursery and go visit his mother and other family members. At this point, you can usually decide to either have the baby stay in your room for all or most of the time, which is called rooming in, or continue to have him go back and forth from the nursery.

Rooming in with your baby can make breastfeeding on demand easier for the mother and give her more time to bond with and understand your baby before going home, but it may make it harder for her to get much rest. Rooming in is also a good idea for Dad, so that he can also bond with the baby and help the mother get some rest.

Nursery workers often assume that sleeping mothers don't want to be awakened for nighttime breast-feedings. If you and your partner don't want your baby to get formula and she isn't rooming in, be sure everyone knows to wake Mom up for feedings and to not give a bottle unless your pediatrician says that it is medically necessary. You should also alert the nursery that you do not want them to use a pacifier, because that can often interfere with effective breastfeeding. (The American Academy of Pediatrics suggests waiting to introduce a pacifier until breastfeeding is well established, which usually happens when babies are around one month old. However, once breastfeeding is going well, experts such as First Candle/SIDS Alliance recommend giving your baby a pacifier every time you place him to sleep. Pacifier use has been found to reduce the risk of sudden infant death syndrome.)

It is estimated that three out of every 1,000 children are born with a permanent hearing loss. In the past, hearing loss wasn't detected until the children affected were toddlers and already had speech and communication delays. A new emphasis on early detection of hearing loss and other developmental delays means that you should know very early if your child is born with a hearing loss.

In fact, the recent increase in universal hearing screening of newborns means that your baby is likely to have a hearing test even before leaving the hospital. This early detection can lead to early intervention and help your child learn to communicate well. Unfortunately, not all states have laws that mandate hearing tests for newborns. If your baby's hearing isn't tested at the hospital, you can ask your pediatrician to schedule a hearing test sometime in your baby's first few months.

Part Two: The First Hours, Days, and Weeks

Bring Your Baby Home

The timing of your baby's discharge from the hospital depends on many things, including how your baby was delivered. Although families often want to leave early (before forty-eight hours), that likely won't be possible if your baby was born by caesarean section. After a C-section, most mothers have to stay in the hospital for three to four days, if not longer.

Discharge Criteria

How well your baby is doing also will be a big factor in the decision as to whether or not she can go home early. Using criteria from the American Academy of Pediatrics, your baby should only be discharged early if she was born full-term, had a normal physical examination, and is maintaining a stable body temperature for at least six to twelve hours.

Before going home, your baby will also have to be either breastfeeding or taking formula well. If your baby isn't latching on, isn't sucking well, or is taking less than an ounce of formula at a time, then she likely will need to spend a little time in the hospital nursery.

Your baby also probably won't be able to go home early if she is much smaller or bigger than the average baby, is having problems with her blood sugar, develops jaundice early, shows any signs of illness, or if the mother had a positive Group B Strep test.

150 Tips and Tricks for New Dads

Even if your baby is doing well, you shouldn't go home until you and her mother are ready. The hospital can be a great resource for you both to learn about breastfeeding, changing diapers, taking a temperature, and so on. Before discharge you also should try to take any parenting classes that the hospital offers.

25 | Learn the Baby Basics

The "basics" are going to mean different things to different people. For a new dad who was never really around a lot of babies before, simply holding a baby is something that will have to be learned. Dads with more experience might need to brush up on other basics, such as feedings, changing diapers, and dressing the baby.

Basics to Learn

The following are some of the more important things that you should know how to do before discharge, so that you will feel more confident and will be able to be more helpful at home.

- Recognize proper breastfeeding techniques, including positioning, latching-on, and sucking
- Prepare your baby's formula and bottles (if using formula)
- Burp your baby
- Change a diaper
- Dress and undress your baby
- Pick up, carry, and hold your baby
- Take a rectal temperature
- Swaddle your baby by snugly wrapping him in a blanket
- Put your baby to sleep on his back to prevent SIDS
- If necessary, care for a circumcised penis

In the first few weeks of breastfeeding, a mom might struggle with nipple soreness, a baby who doesn't latch on well or who has a poor suck, and other problems. Formula-fed babies may not tolerate formula right away, or they may be resistant to certain types.

Breastfeeding Problems

Getting help is easy if you have friends or family members who have breastfed successfully before. If not, look to your pediatrician or a lactation consultant for some expert advice.

Signs that your baby is not breastfeeding well might include:

- Wanting to breastfeed fewer than eight to twelve times in a twenty-four-hour period
- Having fewer than two yellow-green stools by day three or four of life (these follow the black, tarry meconium stools he will have the first two days) or fewer than three to four loose yellow stools by day five to seven
- Having fewer than six full, wet diapers by day five to seven, although urinating less frequently is common until Mom's milk comes in
- Losing more than 5 to 10 percent of his birth weight that first week
- Persistent nipple or breast pain for the mother

Remember that letting your baby breastfeed frequently, at least eight to twelve times a day, is the best way to help Mom establish a good milk supply and encourage effective breastfeeding.

Formula Problems

Although we often think of feeding problems as being limited to those babies who are breastfeeding, formula-fed babies can have problems too. One of the biggest problems is simply not tolerating the formula, which might lead to your having to change to a different type. This means if you are giving your baby a cow's milk–based formula, you might have to switch to a soy or elemental formula.

Is He Gaining Enough Weight?

It is expected that a baby will lose weight during his first week of life. This upsets many parents who were happy with their healthy 7- or 8-pound baby and who don't like to see them drop even an ounce. However, your baby will almost certainly lose at least 5 to 10 percent of his birth weight during that first week. This weight loss is mostly because newborns lose excessive fluid they are born with and because at first they can't eat enough to keep up with their caloric needs.

It used to be that you didn't have a choice in what type of diaper to use, because everyone used cloth diapers. Then everyone started using disposable diapers, and using cloth diapers wasn't a popular option anymore. But now, even though most people use disposables, you have a choice of which type of diaper to use, especially if you live in a bigger city that has a diaper service so that you don't have to wash them yourself.

Disposables or Cloth?

Both disposable and cloth diapers have improved to the point that either could be used for the average baby. The main benefits of using cloth diapers are that they can be less expensive if you clean them yourself and they don't end up in a landfill like disposables do. The downside is that they don't always absorb wetness as well as disposables do, and you can sometimes have more leakage of urine and stool from them. On the other hand, some parents report fewer diaper rashes from cloth diapers. Just determine which type fits better into your overall lifestyle and needs, and understand that either can work for your baby.

It's Changing Time!

When your baby needs a diaper change, get all of your supplies together. This will include a clean diaper,

Part Two: The First Hours, Days, and Weeks

diaper wipes (or a wet washcloth if your baby's skin is too sensitive for wipes), and any diaper rash creams, ointments, or powders you might need.

Diapers that are only wet are easy to change. Simply remove the wet diaper, clean your baby gently with the wipes or washcloth, and then put a clean diaper on the baby. If your baby had a bowel movement, things will be a little more complicated, as you quickly try to get the diaper changed without making a mess all over your baby and yourself. Instead of taking the diaper off all of the way, it can be better to undo it, and then use the top half of the diaper to wipe the bowel movement into the bottom half. There will be much less of the bowel movement left over to clean with the wipes if you do it this way.

If your baby boy was circumcised, be sure to follow any instructions you were given about the care of his circumcised penis when changing his diaper. For girls, remember to always wipe from front to back, so that you don't push any stool into the vaginal area, which can cause irritation and infections.

Developing jaundice, which is a yellowish discoloration to the skin, is very common in newborns. This jaundice typically develops on the baby's second or third day, so it may not be seen in the hospital. Jaundice that develops within twenty-four hours of your baby's birth, or which rapidly gets worse, can be a sign of a more serious problem than the typical "physiological jaundice" that most other babies have.

Jaundice usually starts on your baby's face and in her eyes and then spreads down her body as it gets worse. You should notify your pediatrician if the jaundice seems to be spreading quickly or has already reached your baby's arms and legs. Although many babies with jaundice are simply observed or are placed in indirect sunlight, some babies require blood testing and treatment with phototherapy and special lights. Because so many people are aware of this problem, jaundice rarely gets to a high enough level to cause serious or permanent problems anymore.

Jaundice is not always normal, though. Some conditions, including blood and liver disorders, cannot always simply be observed until they go away. That is why it is a good idea to talk to your pediatrician when your baby is jaundiced, especially if he has other symptoms.

Part Two: The First Hours, Days, and Weeks

Continue to Care for Your Other Children

In some ways, already having children can make having a new baby easy. After all, you are likely to already feel comfortable holding a small baby and may already know how to change a diaper. You may also already have a lot of the clothing and other baby accessories you will need, such as a crib, changing table, and infant carrier. And your baby's mother might already be a pro at breastfeeding.

That said, having other kids at home also adds an extra challenge to the experience of bringing home a new baby. New dads might not be able to stay at the hospital as much as they would like with the new baby because they have to rush home and take care of the other kids. And once you bring the baby home, caring for your other children will leave both Mom and Dad with less time to spend with the new baby.

Another big problem with siblings is the development of jealousy toward the new baby. You can do several things to help prevent this kind of jealousy. These include:

- Preparing siblings for the arrival of the new baby throughout the pregnancy
- Making sure they are being cared for by someone they are comfortable with while you are in the hospital

- Having them at the hospital or at least visiting when the baby is born
- Asking other family members to pay a lot of attention to your other children after you bring your baby home
- Having older siblings help you with simple tasks, such as bringing you a diaper or baby wipe
- Spending "special time" alone with your other children each day, even for just a short time

You should also prepare for and accept regressions in your other children's behavior, although things like tantrums or hitting shouldn't be encouraged, even if your children are upset about the new baby. To be safe, you also shouldn't leave your new baby alone with a young toddler or preschool-age child.

30 Support the New Mom

Once a new mother gets home with her baby, she is likely to be both excited and exhausted. During those first few days after you bring your baby home from the hospital, it is going to be especially important for you to help out. What you actually do to help is going to vary depending on your situation. If your partner had a long or tough delivery or a C-section and is still recovering, then you may have to do a lot more than you ever expected.

How Should You Help?

Even with a quick recovery, you should still help, although that doesn't always mean taking care of the baby. It can sometimes be even more helpful to let the baby's mother spend most of her time bonding with the baby and just take over other household chores yourself. You might care for your other children, do the shopping, clean the house, etc. Helping doesn't always have to mean helping with the baby, unless that is what Mom needs.

If you are still overwhelmed with all that is going on, try to arrange for extra help in the house from other family members or friends. You can ask friends to babysit your other kids, or maybe bring over ready-to-eat meals at least a few times each week. (Just remember to return the favor when they have a new baby!)

Watch for Signs of Postpartum Depression

New dads are often in a good position to recognize the early symptoms of PPD and to offer a lot of help and support so that a new mom doesn't get overwhelmed by all of the things that she is expected to do. Watch for the symptoms of PPD so you can get help for your partner if she needs it. Be aware of a mother who:

- Is crying a lot and feeling sad and depressed most of the time
- Is feeling irritable or restless
- Has no energy
- Is either not eating and is losing weight, or is overeating and gaining a lot of weight
- Has trouble focusing, making decisions, or remembering things
- Feels guilty or worthless
- Is not sleeping well or is overly tired
- Is complaining of a lot of physical symptoms, such as headaches, chest pains, hyperventilation, or heart palpitations
- Is not interested in caring for her baby, or is overly worried that she will hurt the baby
- Has lost interest in her usual activities, or doesn't get any pleasure from them

Part Three

What to Expect in the First Year

The first year of your baby's life are packed with fun "firsts" and developmental milestones. From her first smile to her first step, there will be lots of events you'll want to capture on film. But above and beyond the fun stuff, there is a lot of information you need to navigate these first twelve months. From feeding to safety issues, you should prepare yourself for a busy year of fatherhood!

Get More Sleep

By two and three months old, babies usually still aren't sleeping through the night. They will likely be sleeping for longer and longer stretches of time, though, and they will probably be awake more during the day.

On average, in his second month, a baby is sleeping about fifteen and a half hours a day. And while there may be one stretch of sleep at night that is four to five hours long, many babies are just sleeping for two to three hours at a time and then wanting to eat.

Although the goal for most parents is to help their babies fall asleep on their own and sleep through the night, that isn't going to happen at this age. After six to eight weeks, you can start putting your baby down to sleep while he is drowsy but awake, but in these early months, you might have to rock him to sleep or let him fall asleep breastfeeding. The main early goal is simply to help your baby get into a regular routine of sleeping, ideally with more sleep at night and longer periods of being awake during the day.

If your baby wakes himself frequently when he moves his arms or hands, you might try swaddling him snugly in a light blanket. If you don't feel comfortable firmly folding a blanket around your baby or can't get the swaddling just right, you might buy special swaddling blankets, which are easy to use.

Your baby's early milestones might not sound as important as her later ones, when she will be walking, running, and talking. But these early milestones, like the first smile and first laugh, can be so much more exciting than the ones that happen later.

The milestones that your infant is likely to reach around two or three months old include:

- Smiling by two months
- Looking at or regarding her own hand
- Following objects past the midline of her face
- Laughing, squealing, and saying "ooh" and "aah"
- Being able to hold her head up at a 45° and then 90° angle
- Being able to sit with support and hold her head fairly steady by four months

By the time she reaches the end of her third month, your baby also may be able to bear weight on her legs, roll over, lift herself up on her arms while lying on her chest, grasp a rattle, and hold her hands together. Remember that not all children reach these milestones at the same age, so being a little late can be normal. If your baby is delayed and not catching up after a few weeks or months, or is delayed in more than one area, be sure to talk to your pediatrician.

Get Ready for Growth Spurts

In a baby's first month, growth is fairly predictable. Babies usually lose weight that first week and then slowly start gaining weight until they again reach their birth weight by the time they are two weeks old. For the rest of that first month, most babies continue to gain ½ to 1 ounce each day.

In their second and third months, healthy babies continue to steadily gain weight. But unlike the gradual 1 ounce a day that they gained in the first month, further growth can be a little bit more unpredictable. So they may gain a lot of weight one week and almost none the next, although they will still average about 1 ounce a day and about 5 pounds between one and four months.

It may not seem important to understand these growth spurts and slowdowns, because you won't be weighing your baby that often, but it can help you to understand any increases or decreases in her feedings. During a growth spurt, your baby will likely want to breastfeed more often or drink more formula. Likewise, during a slowdown, she may not want to eat as much. Be sure to see your pediatrician if your baby isn't eating well for more than a few days or if she has a lot of other symptoms, such as fever, vomiting, or fussiness.

Parents are usually well aware of the tragedy of infants who die of sudden infant death syndrome (SIDS). And most know how to avoid SIDS, especially that they should put their baby to sleep on his back and not on his stomach. The following are less well-known tips to help reduce your baby's risk of SIDS:

- Avoid side sleeping, which is better than letting your baby sleep on his stomach, but not as safe as back sleeping.
- Make sure that all caregivers know to put your baby to sleep on his back.
- Don't let your baby get overheated.
- Don't let anyone smoke around your baby.
- Give your baby a pacifier each time you put him to bed, after breastfeeding is well established.

A safe crib, in addition to helping avoid injuries, can also help avoid SIDS. Features of a safe crib include a firm mattress with a tight-fitting crib sheet, slats no more than $2\,^3/_8$ inches apart, and no soft objects, such as fluffy blankets, comforters, pillows, or toys. If you are using a blanket instead of a sleeper, tuck it under the mattress so that it only covers your baby up to his chest. Then place your baby to sleep with his feet near the end that has the blanket tucked under it to make sure that the blanket can't cover your baby's face.

Remember Tummy Time

The important advice to put an infant to sleep on her back means that she is on her stomach for only short periods of time or sometimes not at all. In addition to causing a flat head, this can cause an infant to be delayed in reaching some of her milestones, such as rolling over and crawling. Although even a baby who is hardly ever on her stomach will eventually reach these milestones, daily tummy time can help ensure that she won't be late.

In practicing daily tummy time, you simply put your baby on her stomach for short periods of time when she is awake. To make this more enjoyable, you can get down on the floor with your baby, or use some tummy-time toys, such as a playmat or gym. If your baby cries the whole time that she is on her tummy, limit each time to just a few minutes or wait a few weeks and then try again.

Although studies have shown that some infants do have delayed development if they sleep only on their back, it is not a permanent effect. And while they may pick up milestones later than infants who sleep on their stomach, they still reach those milestones at what is considered to be a normal time.

Before a baby becomes mobile, if you put her down in a safe place, you can usually assume that she will stay safe. Everything changes once she begins rolling around, though, and this often starts well before parents expect it. Parents who wait until they actually see their baby roll over before they start being careful to not leave her alone on a bed, changing table, or the couch are likely to see the baby suffer at least one fall. Keep in mind that the first time your baby rolls over might also be the first time that she rolls off of your bed.

Babies typically begin rolling over between two and six months, but because those are averages and some babies roll over even earlier, it is a good idea to never leave your baby alone in any place where she can roll off and fall.

Go Back to Work

Whenever you go back to work, try to plan things in advance. If neither you nor your partner will be staying home during the day, are you comfortable with the arrangements you have made for a caregiver? Will there be enough help at home to get everything done and still have enough time to get some rest so that you can function at work? If your baby's mother is the one going back to work, be as supportive as you can, and help her to make the necessary plans.

Going back to work and separating from their baby can be stressful for many new mothers and fathers. That makes it important to watch out for, and get help dealing with, increased stress and frustration at this time. Dads should also review the signs of postpartum depression, which might be triggered or worsened when a mother goes back to work.

If you or your partner are not ready to go back to work, look at all of your options to see if it would be possible to stay home a little longer. Maybe you could use up some sick leave or come to some other agreement with your employer. Or perhaps you could just go back part-time. Be realistic about your family's needs, both emotional and financial.

The average infant gets his first tooth at about six months, but the timing of this event varies quite a bit. Some babies get teeth earlier or later, and some are even born with natal teeth. You can usually expect that your baby will get his first tooth sometime between three and fifteen months.

Because the timing of teething is largely genetic, you can sometimes predict when your baby's first tooth will erupt if you know when other family members got their first teeth. If a baby's parents or siblings didn't get their first teeth until eleven or twelve months, then you can expect that your baby won't get his first tooth until later too. If everyone was teething early, then he might too.

Most parents suspect that their baby is teething at around three or four months when he starts drooling a lot and wants to chew on things. While it is possible for a baby to get his first tooth that early, in most cases those aren't signs of teething. Instead, those are normal physical and developmental milestones that most children begin at this age, whether or not they are teething.

Still, your baby may start drooling more and want to chew on things when he really does start teething. The key to figuring out whether or not he is teething is to look for other signs and symptoms. Is he a little fussier than usual? Can you see or feel his first tooth coming through? Do his gums look red or swollen? All of those things can be associated with teething, which typically begins as the bottom two middle teeth, the central incisors, erupt.

After your baby gets his first tooth, he will usually continue to get three or four more teeth every three or four months. This will continue until he gets all twenty of his baby teeth at around age two and a half years.

You don't necessarily need to brush these first teeth, but you do need to clean them. A moist washcloth or a piece of soft gauze can be used to wipe them clean before bed each night. Once your child gets several more teeth, you can use a soft infant's toothbrush instead.

You probably don't have to start using toothpaste until your baby gets a few more teeth. And once you do, be sure to use a nonfluoride toothpaste until your child is old enough to spit out the toothpaste. Swallowing too much of a fluoride toothpaste can cause fluorosis and staining on his teeth.

The timing of the first visit to the dentist is controversial. The American Academy of Pediatric Dentists recommends a visit once your baby gets his first tooth. And that's not a bad idea. An early visit to the dentist can help to identify problems and educate parents in proper tooth care to avoid later problems.

The American Academy of Pediatrics (AAP) used to recommend a later visit, around age three. It now recommends an earlier visit, especially if your child has any risk factors for developing problems with his teeth, such as frequent nighttime feedings. Infants who already have cavities should also see a pediatric dentist. Whether or not you see a dentist, the AAP recommends that your pediatrician examine and review your child's oral health at each well-child visit.

Part Three: What to Expect in the First Year

Watch for More Milestones Between Months Four and Seven

Big changes are in store for your baby at this age, all of which will help him to become a little more independent. Instead of just lying in one position, he will now be able to roll over and sit up to observe and interact with the world around him. From four to seven months, the milestones that your child is likely to achieve include:

- Passing a block from one hand to the other
- Reaching for things
- Looking for objects that you drop
- Imitating many speech sounds
- Turning toward a voice
- Talking in single syllables
- Rolling over
- Sitting without support

He also probably will be able to hold his head steady if you try to pull on his arms to get him up to a sitting position. And he may be able to stand by holding on to things, put syllables together, and say "dada" and "mama," although those words won't be used as a label for you or his mother.

Your child's diet is going to change quite a bit during months eight through twelve. In addition to continuing on breastmilk or formula, your child will be eating a lot more baby food at this age. You will be able to start introducing finger foods and table foods, which your baby is sure to enjoy. Your baby also will start feeding himself more.

In addition to single-ingredient cereals, fruits, and vegetables, there will be a lot more variety in your baby's diet at this age. You can now start more multi-ingredient or mixed foods such as rice cereal with applesauce, mixed vegetables, and vegetable beef dinners. Just be sure that your infant has eaten and tolerated all of the ingredients in a multi-ingredient food. For example, if your baby didn't tolerate bananas, then don't give her a banana-apple dessert.

Choose the Right Foods

Your baby should be ready for finger foods once he is sitting up well on his own and is able to pick up things with his thumb and finger and bring them to his mouth. This usually happens at about eight to nine months, although some infants aren't interested in finger foods until a little later. The first finger foods are usually offered as a snack and can include dry cereals such as Cheerios, baby cookies and crackers, and plain wafer cookies. Be sure to always supervise your baby when he is eating and don't offer foods he can choke on, such as whole grapes or raw vegetables. Remember that you don't have to wait until your baby has teeth to start safe types of regular food. As long as you choose foods that are soft and well cooked or that can easily break down in his mouth, he should be able to eat them without teeth.

Once your baby is doing well with textured baby food and finger foods, you can start to offer more regular food that you are eating. You still want to avoid foods that your baby can choke on. Also, don't add a lot of salt or other seasonings to the food. If you do add a lot of seasonings, separate the food that you are going to give your baby from the food that the rest of the family will eat. Table foods that your baby should do well with include cut-up meats, well-cooked vegetables and pasta, and small pieces of cheese and ripe fruits.

Weaning actually has a few different meanings. For breastfeeding babies, it usually means the time when they gradually cut back on breastfeeding with the idea of soon stopping. For bottle babies, weaning is the process of going from a bottle to a cup.

If weaning from breastfeeding, first make sure that both your partner and your baby are ready. And remember that the American Academy of Pediatrics (AAP) recommendation to breastfeed until twelve months is a minimum and not a limit on how long to breastfeed. If Mom and baby both want to, your baby can continue to breastfeed after his first birthday. Once your baby does start weaning, try to let him do it gradually, eliminating one feeding every few days or weeks.

You should usually wean from a bottle just as slowly. You can make it easier if you offer juice and water in a cup only. That way, when you switch from formula to cow's milk when your baby is a year old and make the transition to using a cup, he will already be used to it.

Finally, be aware that there is such a thing as a nursing strike. Most babies wean slowly, dropping one feeding every few days or weeks. If your baby refuses most or all of her feedings all of a sudden, then it is more likely to be a nursing strike than weaning, which means that she should be able to continue breastfeeding once she gets over whatever is bothering her.

Part Three: What to Expect in the First Year

Watch for Your Baby's First Steps

Your baby's first steps are one of the bigger milestones that most dads anticipate. Sure, it's exciting when your baby first rolls over or sits up, but beginning to walk is even more exciting. Few other milestones provoke calls to the grandparents and a rush to get the video camera.

Cruising

Before your baby learns to walk, she will begin cruising around, or walking while holding on to things. This usually begins at around nine or ten months, once your baby is able to get to a sitting and then standing position by herself. She will quickly become more adventurous, walking while holding furniture, your hand, or her push toys.

Once your baby is cruising around effortlessly, you might think that she will quickly be walking. For some infants that's true, but for others it can take four or five months for them to walk well. On average, babies are walking on their own by ten to fifteen months. Talk to your pediatrician if your baby isn't walking by that time.

Learning to walk is just one of the big milestones that infants pick up at this age. Your baby will soon seem all grown up as she begins talking, playing, and exploring the world around her.

Listen for Baby Talk

Although your baby probably won't pick up more than a few words by twelve months, you will begin to hear what sounds like a whole new language. After mastering single syllables, she will quickly begin putting syllables together and jabbering away. She will also begin saying "mama" and "dada" between six and nine months, although it won't be specifically to call you or her mom until she is about fourteen months old.

Next, she will begin saying a few other words, such as ball or cat. Some babies don't say their first word, other than mama and dada, until about fifteen to eighteen months. If you are concerned about your baby's language development, be sure to talk to your pediatrician to find out if she needs to have her hearing checked or needs an early childhood intervention referral.

Watch Him Play

As your baby is getting more interested in things and becoming more social, he also is more fun to play with. You likely always had fun playing with him when he was younger, but you often just got to see the reaction he had to what you were doing. Maybe you made him laugh, smile, or reach for things, but he didn't really participate very much.

Now you can expect your child to really play more. He should be able to roll a ball back to you and push toy cars around. He will also begin to enjoy simple cloth and cardboard books and being read to as you hold him on your lap. Other fun games can include peek-a-boo, and he will likely enjoy stacking ring cones and nesting cups.

Be on the Lookout for Other Milestones

While your baby was only rolling around just a few months ago, interested only in mouth toys, by eight to twelve months she is now developing complex behaviors to explore her world. These include the concept of object permanence, which is the idea that things still exist even if you can't see them anymore. She will also be developing object mastery, as she learns to operate and play with more complicated toys with buttons, levers, and doors. The milestones that will help her develop these new patterns of behavior include:

- Beginning to wave "bye-bye" by seven months (some kids don't do this until fourteen months)
- Letting you know what she wants, such as by pointing to things
- Picking up things with her finger and thumb in a pincer grasp
- Putting things that she picks up into her mouth
- Banging objects together
- Being able to pull up to a standing position and get to a sitting position by ten months
- Looking for things that move out of her sight by eleven months
- Responding to simple one-step commands and the word "no" by eleven or twelve months

Your baby also may begin to imitate things that you are doing and will soon be able to scribble on paper, use a spoon and fork to eat, stack blocks on top of each other, walk backward, and run. With your twelve-month well-child visit coming up at the end of this time period, now is a good time to list any concerns you have about your child's development. That way you will be prepared to discuss them with your pediatrician and get some help if it is needed.

Part Four

Your Pediatrician

For many parents, their pediatrician is one of the people they have the most contact with outside the house during their baby's first year. That makes choosing a good one important. Having a pediatrician you feel comfortable with will also help you feel confident that your child is growing and developing normally and that you are making the right choices about his care.

Understand How Pediatricians Are Trained

It can help you to understand your pediatrician and develop a better relationship if you realize how many years of training that he had to go through to learn how to take care of your child. Your child's doctor endured many years of school, training, and sleepless nights before becoming a pediatrician.

Training for a pediatrician begins with four years of college, followed by four years of medical school, and then three years in a pediatric internship and residency program. These eleven years of training leave most pediatricians well prepared to recognize and treat common pediatric problems as well as provide guidance to help you raise happy and healthy children.

In addition to graduating from each of these programs, your pediatrician had to pass three steps of the United States Medical Licensing Examination to get his medical license, and also had to pass an exam from the American Board of Pediatrics to become board certified in pediatrics.

A pediatrician's training doesn't end there. Even after eleven years of preparation and all of those exams, your pediatrician also has to complete training each year to get Continuing Medical Education credits. This training includes attending medical conferences as well as other lectures and courses, where health professionals learn about the latest medical discoveries and treatments.

Deciding which pediatrician you will trust with the care of your new baby is a big decision, and it is one that is made differently by different parents. Although there might not be one best way to choose a good pediatrician that you will be happy with, there are some things that you should *not* do.

- Don't just pick a doctor from the phone book or from a list provided by your insurance company.
- Don't pick whoever is on-call when your baby is born.
- Don't go to a doctor just because the office is in a convenient location.

It is important to choose a pediatrician before your baby is born so that if anything goes wrong, you will know who is taking care of your baby and advising you on medical decisions that you must make.

Also remember that even with a lot of recommendations and a good prenatal visit, it will still take a few "real-world" visits to find out if you have found the right pediatrician for you. It could be that there is a policy you didn't know about, or maybe the doctor was simply on her best behavior for the interview. If you later encounter problems and you can't resolve them, start the process over and look for another pediatrician.

Part Four: Your Pediatrician

Get Recommendations

Your choice is fairly easy if you already have a pediatrician who has been caring for your other children or if your own pediatrician is still practicing. If not, the best way to find a pediatrician is to get recommendations from friends or family members who have pediatricians that they like. But it is important to find out *why* they like their doctors. Is it simply because the office is efficient and they can get in and out quickly? Or is it because they always get an antibiotic when they want one?

When accepting someone's recommendation, make sure that you are comfortable with the reason why they like the pediatrician, and that this reason has something to do with being an educated and competent doctor (not a personal preference for the way the waiting room is decorated, for instance). The same applies when a person recommends against a doctor, because the reason for being unhappy with that particular pediatrician may be something that wouldn't bother you. Your partner's own ob/gyn might also be a good source of a recommendation, but again, ask why she is recommending the pediatrician.

It is important to consider your own expectations when you choose a pediatrician. Do you want to always be able to talk to the doctor when you call for advice, and not have to speak with a nurse? Do you expect these calls to be able to last fifteen or thirty minutes?

If you have moved or your previous pediatrician is no longer practicing, you can't always expect to have the same relationship with your new doctor. Just because your previous pediatrician gave you her home phone number to use at any time does not mean that your new pediatrician will do the same thing. The one thing you should expect is that building a relationship takes time on both ends, although with time you may get those same privileges from another doctor.

Although parents often focus on office hours, hospital affiliations, and length of wait times, one of the most important things to focus on is the pediatrician's style of practicing medicine. Does he wear a white coat and tie and seem very formal, or does he dress casually and have a playful, informal style? Does he spend a long time explaining things, or does he provide you with reference material that you can take home and read? What are your preferences? Recognizing the pediatrician's style is important. There will likely be a particular pediatrician's style with which you and your baby's mother will be most comfortable.

Part Four: Your Pediatrician

As you look for a pediatrician, you will notice that some doctors practice all by themselves in a solo practice, while others work with a large group of other doctors. While it shouldn't be the most important factor when you choose a pediatrician, you should understand some of the differences between solo and group practice pediatricians, as well as the major pros and cons of each.

Solo Practice Pediatricians

One of the main benefits of going to a pediatrician in practice by himself is that when you have a visit, you will always see your pediatrician. You don't have to worry about explaining your child's whole medical history to another doctor or seeing someone you don't necessarily like or trust. Even when you call after-hours, you will get to talk to your own doctor.

Another benefit is that a small office will have a small staff. That means that the receptionist, nurses, and office manager are likely to recognize you when you come in and better understand your family's specific needs. You will probably also be able to get common tasks, such as getting a copy of your child's immunization records, done quickly.

Of course, such a small office can be a problem if you don't like or get along with even one of the office's staff members. Another downside is that without any other doctors covering for your pediatrician, you may not always get an appointment when you want one. A small office also may not have the latest medical technology available, so you might have to go elsewhere for simple lab tests and other procedures.

Group Practice Pediatricians

A pediatrician in a group practice shares an office with one or more other pediatricians. With more doctors being available, you probably will be able to get an appointment whenever you want one. You may not be able to see your own doctor or talk to your own doctor after-hours, though.

Another downside is that with a larger office, there will be more office staff and you may not get to know everyone in the office. However, a larger office will have more resources, and it will likely be able to provide more services than a solo practitioner will.

51 Think about Practical Matters

Once you've decided what kind of practice you're interested in, there are some less prominent, yet no less important, details to consider. Before making your final choice of a pediatrician, you should consider the following practical matters:

- Is the pediatrician on your insurance plan?
- Is he or she in a convenient location so that you don't have to drive for an hour with a sick child?
- Are the office hours convenient for you?
- How long do you have to wait for an appointment?
- Will you always see your own pediatrician?
- How long will you be kept waiting in the office?
- Is someone available when the office is closed if you need help?
- Is the office affiliated with a children's hospital?

Although you could wait until your prenatal visit to consider these questions, you could also do a little homework on your own and call the offices to save some time. These are also great questions to ask of friends and family about the pediatricians they might be recommending to you.

You wouldn't hire a new employee without interviewing her first, or move into a new house without seeing and inspecting it beforehand, and likewise, you shouldn't choose a pediatrician before you've met and interviewed him.

Although the first visit with a pediatrician is often called a "new mom consult," it is usually best if both Mom and Dad go to any prenatal visits to meet the doctors that you are considering. After you make a list of candidates from recommendations and the questions found in this chapter, try to schedule a prenatal visit to meet each doctor. While some doctors charge for these "interviews," most provide them as a free service.

You will want to ask several questions about issues that are important to you, but the main point of these visits is simply to find out if you feel comfortable with the pediatrician and to see how his office works. For example, if you see a waiting room that is overflowing with frustrated parents who seem to be waiting for long periods of time, you might end up waiting for your visits, too, unless there was an emergency that put the office behind schedule. If you show up early for your prenatal visit and see a regular stream of kids come in and quickly go back to see the doctor, then you have likely found an office that is run very efficiently and which you might want to go to yourself.

Get Educated about Specialists

The average pediatrician is well trained to help with all of the problems new parents face, from advice about day-to-day basics, such as feeding and sleep issues, to caring for your baby when he is sick. There may, however, be times when your baby needs more care than your pediatrician can provide.

Many pediatric specialists are also pediatricians. After completing their general pediatric training, they then go on to do a three-year fellowship and get their specialist training. These types of specialists include, among others, pediatric cardiologists, endocrinologists, gastroenterologists, hematologists, and pulmonologists. There also are pediatric specialists in genetics, nephrology, neurology, emergency medicine, and infectious disease.

Your pediatrician can help you choose the specialist who would be best to see your child when and if it becomes necessary.

Many other health-care professionals who are not doctors can help take care of your child's health-care needs. These include speech, occupational, and physical therapists to manage and treat developmental delays, and lactation consultants to help with breast-feeding problems.

One of the most common reasons to see a specialist is because your pediatrician thinks that it is necessary. Another reason, though, is simply because you want a second opinion. You might disagree with your pediatrician, either because she is being too aggressive or not aggressive enough, or you may just feel more comfortable and better reassured with a specialist's opinion.

Although getting a second opinion from a specialist should be an easy process, you might encounter a few potential roadblocks. Two common problems are that there may not be a specialist available in your area or there might be a long waiting list to see the doctors who are around. In either situation, you might ask your pediatrician to call a specialist to get further advice about what to do for your child.

Another problem might be that your pediatrician simply refuses to refer you to a specialist. You shouldn't have to beg for a referral, and if your pediatrician can't convince you that it isn't necessary, then you might want to go to a different pediatrician. Last, your insurance company might refuse to authorize the referral. A letter of medical necessity from your pediatrician should be enough to override this refusal, though you may have to ask about an appeal process to get the referral approved.

Know When to Call Your Pediatrician

It is especially important to call if your baby has any of the following symptoms:

- A rectal temperature of 100.4°F or above (when the baby is less than three months old)
- A temperature above 101°F (from three to six months)
- A temperature above 103°F (after six months)
- Trouble breathing
- Fussiness that doesn't improve when you hold her, especially if she also has a fever, poor appetite, or other symptoms
- Projectile vomiting or vomiting up a dark green substance
- Vomiting and/or diarrhea causing dehydration
- Bloody diarrhea
- Poor appetite, not eating well
- Excessive sleeping or difficulty waking up
- Problems breastfeeding to the point at which you need to supplement more than you want to

It is hard to have specific guidelines about when to call if your older infant has a fever, so even if your seven-month-old has just a low-grade fever of 101°F and you are concerned, call your pediatrician. You should also trust your instincts and call any other time that you think your baby is ill and you need help.

It's important to make good use of the time you have in your pediatrician's office, because your pediatrician will also be busy with lots of other patients. You also may be tired or distracted when you're in the waiting room and therefore might not have the presence of mind or the opportunity to think about important questions and discussion points to bring up. Preparing a list of questions beforehand can help ensure that you don't forget anything important.

In addition to preparing a list of questions well before your visit, you also need to consider more practical matters. The first step in preparing for your visits to the doctor is deciding who actually is going to take your baby to the office. Will it be Mom, Dad, a grandparent, or another caregiver?

Although you often don't have much choice because of work schedules and other constraints, ideally both Mom and Dad would go to each visit. That way each parent can ask his or her own questions and get a better understanding of how the baby is growing and developing. Don't leave the office until you both feel that you've had all your questions sufficiently answered.

Part Four: Your Pediatrician

57 Know How Often a Baby Needs Checkups

You will make a lot of visits to your pediatrician for checkups during your baby's first year. These check-ups, or well-child visits, include an evaluation of your baby's growth, development, and feeding habits; a complete physical examination; a discussion of what you should be doing to take care of your baby's needs; and usually some vaccines. Because appointments for well-child visits are planned far in advance, both parents should make every effort to attend.

Most pediatricians stick to a standard timing schedule for well-child visits as recommended by the American Academy of Pediatrics. This schedule calls for visits at the following ages:

- Two weeks
- Two months
- Four months
- Six months
- Nine months
- Twelve months

If your baby was discharged home early from the hospital (fewer than forty-eight hours after being born), then your first visit to your pediatrician should be within another twenty-four to forty-eight hours. This is especially important if your baby is breastfeeding.

When attending a well-child visit, be prepared to answer the following questions about your baby:

- How often is he breastfeeding or taking a bottle of formula?
- What new foods have you introduced since the last visit?
- What new milestones has your baby picked up, such as rolling over, sitting up, or standing?
- How well is he sleeping at night and for his naps?
- In what position is he sleeping?
- Where is he sitting in the car, and in what kind of car seat?
- Has he had any reactions to his immunizations?
- Are you giving him a vitamin or any other medications?
- What concerns do you have about his development?

Be prepared so that your baby's doctor can more easily determine how well your child is doing. Questions you might ask your doctor include which foods to start next, what milestones to watch for, and what things you should avoid doing.

59 Learn What to Expect at a Sick-Child Visit

You should usually expect a same-day appointment when your child is sick, unless your child's condition is a long-term or nonurgent problem, such as acne or bowlegs. It is unreasonable to expect a parent or child to wait even one or two days when the infant has an ear infection, fever, or difficulty breathing. You probably should look for another doctor if you are regularly made to wait several days for appointments when your baby is sick.

Some questions that you should be prepared to answer during each sick visit include:

- How long has your child been sick?
- What are all of his symptoms?
- When are the symptoms worse?
- How have the symptoms been changing?
- What makes the symptoms better?
- How has being sick affected his eating and sleeping?
- Has he been around anyone else who's been sick?
- What medications have you been giving him?
- Why do you think he hasn't been getting better?
- What are you most worried about with this illness?

Parents seem to have a million questions that they want to ask their pediatrician, but they often forget them during the visit. Preparing a list of questions and bringing them to your visits can help to make sure that you get all of your questions answered. Some good questions to start with at a sick visit include:

- What is my child's diagnosis?
- What causes this?
- What treatments are you prescribing, if any?
- What are the side effects of those treatments?
- Are there any alternatives to those treatments?
- When should he start getting better?
- What are some signs to watch for that might mean he is getting worse?
- When can he return to day care?
- Do I have to limit his diet or activity?
- Should I bring him back for a recheck?

Getting answers to these questions (and making note of the answers) is especially helpful if only one parent can make it to the visit and needs to explain everything to the other.

Part Four: Your Pediatrician

Part Five

Infant Nutrition

What and how much to feed a baby is one of the things that many parents have trouble with, especially if they are getting a lot of differing advice on when to start solids, how long to breastfeed, or what foods to avoid. Being familiar with your baby's nutritional requirements and needs can help so that you have one less thing to worry about.

Encourage Your Partner to Pump Breastmilk

There are many reasons why your partner may want to pump and store her breastmilk for use later on. Some of these reasons include that she may be at work and unable to breastfeed all of the time, or she may have to go on a trip without her baby and isn't ready to wean. Babies are also fed pumped breastmilk if Dad wants to feed his exclusively breastfed baby some of the time or if you get your milk from a human breastmilk bank.

Choose the Right Pump

Many different types of breast pumps are available for your partner, from manually operated hand pumps to hospital-grade electric pumps. There is even a hands-free pump that operates on batteries. Any of these can get the job done, but if your partner is going to be pumping a lot or is pumping to build up her milk supply, you should try to get a hospital-grade pump. These are more expensive, but they often can be rented from a lactation consultant.

It's important to note that a woman should never use someone else's breast pump. Like toothbrushes, pumps are designed for single users. (The only exception to this rule is hospital-grade pumps, which are designed to be used by more than one person. The milk never touches the working parts of the pump that are shared with other mothers.)

The following guidelines from the American Academy of Pediatrics and La Leche League International will help you decide how long you can store pumped breastmilk. According to these guidelines, stored milk can be kept:

- At room temperature for four hours
- In a small refrigerator or cooler until your baby's mom gets home to store it in your refrigerator or freezer
- Unfrozen in a refrigerator for three to eight days
- In a freezer that is in the same compartment as the refrigerator for two weeks
- In a freezer with a separate door from the refrigerator for one to three or four months
- In a chest freezer for six months

Frozen breastmilk can be thawed by moving it into a refrigerator for up to twenty-four hours. Once you are ready to use it, refrigerated breastmilk should be warmed by running it under warm water, and then it should be shaken and put into a bottle or cup for your baby to drink. Similar to formula, expressed breastmilk should not be heated in a microwave oven.

If not breastfeeding, babies usually drink formula throughout their first years. Once they reach their first birthday, they can then usually be switched to whole cow's milk, unless they have a milk allergy or intolerance. What some parents struggle with most is the amount of formula to give each day.

Most babies start out drinking two to three ounces of formula during the first few weeks, with frequent feedings (every three to four hours). By two months, many have moved up to five to six ounces per feeding and have spaced their feedings so that they are only eating five to six times a day. Keep in mind that your baby may drink less more frequently or bigger bottles less often, but she probably will be averaging about twenty-four to thirty-two ounces a day after she is two months old.

While many babies will plateau and continue to drink five to six ounces at a time as they get older, some babies increase their intake to six to seven ounces at each feeding once they are three to five months old. If your baby is consistently drinking much more than that, you might check with your pediatrician to make sure that you are not overfeeding your baby. Although it isn't usually easy to overfeed a baby, because most turn away or spit up if they get overfull, it can happen if you misinterpret when she is actually hungry and feed your baby each time she cries.

The only real alternatives to infant formulas are other infant formulas, such as a soy or elemental formula if your baby is having a problem with a cow's milk–based formula. While formula is a "second best" alternative to breastmilk, by the time you begin having problems with formula feeding, it will likely be too late to breastfeed. If you do begin to have formula problems early on or while your baby is still breastfeeding a little, especially within the first week or so after being born, you might talk to a lactation consultant to help get your baby exclusively breastfeeding and avoid formula altogether.

Homemade infant formula, goat's milk, and cow's milk are poor alternatives to a commercially prepared iron-fortified infant formula and should be avoided. None of them offer any advantages over formula, and in fact they can lead to vitamin and mineral deficiencies, gastrointestinal disturbances, and other problems.

Once your baby is doing well with a formula, you should usually stick to it for the rest of your baby's first year. Although formula for older infants is being marketed, most children don't need the extra calcium and other vitamins and minerals in these formulas, because they can get them from the baby foods they are eating.

Part Five: Infant Nutrition

Don't Worry about Nutrition Rules

Parents often want detailed rules for how much to feed their baby. How many ounces does he need each day or during each feeding? How often should he eat? What should they be feeding him?

Unfortunately, there aren't any formal rules that specify what each and every child should be eating. Just as kids come in different shapes and sizes, they also have different appetites and nutritional needs. One baby might only drink twenty-four ounces of formula a day, while another needs thirty-two or even forty ounces a day. Or one six-month-old might be eating two meals a day, with cereal, vegetables, and fruits, while another is just barely starting cereal. And all of these kids, with their very different diets, could be growing and developing just fine. So instead of looking for strict rules, parents should follow more general guidelines, and simply make sure that their baby is satisfied and growing well.

It's no fun having a child with food allergies. In addition to the fear of serious, life-threatening reactions, it can be a struggle to simply know what is safe to feed him. Complicating matters is the fact that food children are commonly allergic to, such as milk, eggs, soy, and wheat, can be hidden ingredients in many other foods.

To try to avoid food allergies, some parents delay giving certain foods that kids commonly are allergic to, such as peanuts, cow's milk, and eggs. While those foods should usually be avoided during your baby's first year anyway, after that, it may not be necessary to avoid them if your baby doesn't have any risk factors for food allergies. Still, as long as your toddler eats a well-balanced diet, delaying some foods isn't going to hurt him, and it might be a good idea if you are really worried about food allergies.

If your baby has risk factors for food allergies, such as having formula allergies, other types of allergic disorders such as eczema or asthma, or has a family member with food allergies or other allergic disorders, you may be able to reduce his chance of developing a food allergy by making sure he:

- Breastfeeds exclusively for at least six months
- Continues to breastfeed until he is at least twelve months old

Part Five: Infant Nutrition

- Drinks a hypoallergenic formula if he is being supplemented or isn't breastfeeding
- Doesn't begin solid foods until six months
- Doesn't eat or drink any dairy products until he is twelve months old
- Doesn't eat eggs until he is two years old
- Doesn't eat peanuts or peanut butter, nuts, or fish until he is three years old

You can reduce your baby's risk even more if the mother doesn't eat nuts while breastfeeding. The need to eliminate other foods, such as cow's milk, eggs, and fish, from a nursing mother's diet is more controversial.

Most parents know not to give honey to their baby in the first year, but it is also important to avoid foods made with honey. This includes honey cereals and honey graham crackers, a popular finger food among some parents. If a food has honey in it, and it is not pasteurized, then you should avoid it until your baby is older so that you don't risk his getting botulism.

Most parents look forward to starting solid foods, because it is a fun thing to do for both them and their baby. For a dad with a breastfeeding baby, starting solids can be especially rewarding because it lets dad be a bigger part of his baby's feedings. Many parents start too early, though.

Although the general guidelines are that you can start solids anytime between four and six months, you can usually wait until six months. You may have a good reason to start early if your baby is no longer satisfied with just breastmilk or formula. Make sure, though, that you aren't confusing a growth spurt and a few days of increased feedings for a need to start solid foods. Other things to look for include that your baby has doubled her birth weight and is no longer trying to push solid foods out of her mouth with her tongue.

Don't Introduce Foods Too Quickly

In addition to starting too early, the other mistake some parents make when feeding solid foods is offering too many foods too quickly. It's easy to see why this happens; parents are often eager to see what their child likes and dislikes. But if you offer too many new foods too quickly, such as by introducing bananas one day and peaches the next, and your baby has a problem, it won't be easy to know which food is causing the problem. Instead, you should offer one new food every two to three days and don't offer combination foods or mixed cereals until your baby has eaten all of the ingredients separately. This is one experience in which patience is definitely a virtue.

Once you know that your baby is ready for solid foods, knowing what to start with is easy. In almost all cases, the best first food to start with is an iron-fortified, single-grain rice cereal. Rice cereal is usually the best tolerated and the least likely to cause allergies or other problems.

The first time you start cereal, you probably will have to make it very thin, by mixing one teaspoon of cereal with four or five teaspoons of expressed breastmilk, formula, or water. And don't expect your baby to eat a lot of it. At first, she may eat just one or two teaspoons a day, and a lot of that might end up all over her face. If she doesn't want it at all, try again in a few days. It might also help to make sure she isn't overly hungry when you offer cereal, by giving it after a feeding or after at least a few minutes of breastfeeding or a few ounces of formula.

Once your baby is eating rice cereal well, you can either begin offering other cereals, such as oatmeal or barley, or just stick with rice. You can eventually mix your baby's cereal with less liquid as she gets more used to the thicker texture, and work your way up to three to five tablespoons of cereal a day.

Move Up to Vegetables and Fruits

Once your baby has mastered cereal, you can offer single-ingredient baby food, such as pureed vegetables and fruits. She will likely just start out with one to two tablespoons once or twice a day and then later move up to two to three tablespoons at a time.

Once your baby is eating two to three meals a day, consisting of three to five tablespoons of cereal and two to three tablespoons of vegetables and fruits, he will likely be ready for some meat and protein foods. This will usually occur when your baby is about eight months old. Remember that he will still have three to five feedings of breastmilk and formula in addition to the solid foods.

By eight to nine months, or once your baby is sitting up well, he should be ready for some finger foods, such as Cheerios, crackers, and arrowroot cookies. At this age, he is also likely to be ready for foods with more texture, such as Stage 3 baby foods.

Iron is one of the more important minerals your baby needs. Your infant, unless he was born premature, should be able to get all of the iron he needs from breastmilk or an iron-fortified formula during his first four to six months. After that time he does need extra iron, but you can usually provide it from the baby foods that he is beginning to eat, such as an iron-fortified infant rice cereal, in addition to continuing to feed him his breastmilk or formula.

Newborns don't need fluoride, but once your infant is about six months old and begins getting teeth, he will need fluoride to keep them strong and growing well. The main source of this fluoride isn't an extra vitamin though. You can instead provide it by offering your baby some fluoridated tap water each day.

Not getting enough vitamin D can cause a baby to get a bone disorder called rickets. Because infant formula is fortified with vitamin D, infants drinking at least seventeen ounces of formula each day do not need any extra vitamin D. Breastmilk does not contain enough vitamin D for babies, so the American Academy of Pediatrics now recommends that breastfed babies receive a vitamin D supplement beginning in the first two months of life.

Part Five: Infant Nutrition

Deal with Food Strikes

Babies who refuse to eat can be frustrating to take care of, especially if they don't want to drink their breastmilk or formula. If your baby had previously been eating well and all of a sudden decides not to eat as much, he may just be at the end of a growth spurt or is having a short "strike." Other causes for a baby not wanting to eat can include gastroesophageal reflux and a food aversion, which often affects older infants who won't eat solid foods.

This situation is more concerning if the food refusal lasts more than a few days or if your baby has other symptoms, such as increased fussiness or fever. If there are any other symptoms or if the food refusal lingers, a trip to your pediatrician is a good idea.

Most kids like drinking juice. Whether they are thirsty, hungry, or simply crying because they are angry, infants rarely turn away a bottle of juice when it is offered to them. This can lead some parents to start using juice as a pacifier, creating a bad habit that is hard to break.

To avoid negative health effects, such as becoming overweight or getting cavities, you should follow these juice recommendations from the American Academy of Pediatrics (AAP):

- Don't give juice to infants under six months old.
- Limit juice intake to four to six ounces a day.
- Only give pasteurized 100 percent fruit juices (instead of fruit drinks).
- Don't give juice in a bottle.

The AAP's recommendation to avoid unpasteurized fruit juices really only applies to commercial sources of juices, which might contain harmful bacteria if not pasteurized. Therefore, making your own juice using fresh fruit can be a healthful alternative to other drinks.

You might also dilute the juice with water when you do give it to your older infant and avoid giving infants juice at bedtime or in the middle of the night. And it can be helpful to have designated times, either at meals or snacks, for your child to have juice.

Part Five: Infant Nutrition

Avoid Junk Food Addiction

Obesity levels are rising to epidemic levels in children and adults. Although you shouldn't limit your child's calories or intake of fat, it is never too early to start offering nutritious choices and a diet that's healthful overall.

Early infancy is probably the time when you have the most control over what your child eats. After all, a nine-month-old can't go to the pantry to get a cookie or to the refrigerator to get a soda. Sure, she might cry if she doesn't get what she wants, but you still have control over what you give her to eat.

In addition to too much juice, one of the biggest sources of junk food in an infant's diet is the type of finger foods you give her to snack on. Foods to avoid include sugary cereal and other typical junk foods, such as sugary cookies, chips, or doughnuts. Soft, small pieces of fruits and vegetables, plain wafer cookies, and low-sugar cereals are better options.

Once you let your baby start eating table foods, your own choices, if they are unhealthy, can begin to affect your child's diet. Choosing healthy finger foods, not giving too much juice, and offering a variety of healthful foods at meals can help you avoid creating a junk-food junkie.

Kids can be picky eaters because they are drinking too much formula or juice or eating a lot of junk food, and then simply aren't hungry when it's time for dinner. On the other hand, some picky eaters just don't want to eat a variety of foods. A child who is really just a "natural" picky eater—one who eats small amounts of food or has little variety in her diet but has no bad habits—probably is normal, especially if she is gaining weight normally and is physically active. It can still be frustrating when your child refuses to eat most of the things that you offer her, though, so you should try to avoid actually creating a picky eater.

Picky eaters who are truly created are more likely to live in homes where other family members also aren't good eaters. Most older infants welcome a variety of foods, and they are eager to eat new things from the plates of other family members. The family of a picky eater may not eat many fruits and vegetables or may not like to try new foods, offering little variety at each meal. In addition to offering your child a variety of healthful foods, including fruits and vegetables, it is important that other family members also eat and enjoy a variety of foods to avoid creating a picky eater.

Part Six

All about Sleep

With all of the other things to be concerned about during your baby's first year—including her overall health, safety, growth, and development—whether or not she is sleeping well may seem like a small problem. However, the parent who is getting by on little or no sleep each night will understand how important it can be to have a baby who is sleeping well.

Learn the Sleep Basics

Early on, instead of long stretches of sleep, your newborn will probably have regular cycles of eating, sleeping, and waking each day. Although there may be one longer stretch of four or five hours, most of these cycles will be just two or three hours. Over the next three or four months, your baby's sleep patterns should become more organized.

Just as your baby's sleep patterns change over this first year, sleep advice also changes. It is important to realize that much of the advice for older children—letting them fall asleep on their own, not letting them fall asleep while feeding, and perhaps letting them cry it out—doesn't apply to your newborn or younger infant. Your newborn probably will fall asleep breastfeeding or drinking a bottle or may need to be rocked to sleep. Helping your child get to sleep in these first few months doesn't mean that you are creating problems for later.

As your baby gets older, you may have to work a little more at preventing and fixing sleep problems that develop, so that all family members can get a healthful amount of sleep. However, for many babies, whether or not they sleep well is just part of who they are naturally. It is possible to create good and bad sleepers, but sometimes you just have to wait and adjust to your child's natural sleep schedule until things work themselves out as the child gets older.

In early infancy, nighttime feedings are to be expected. Your newborn will likely continue to eat every two to three hours at night, just as he does during the day.

Once your baby is gaining weight well, it is fine if he wants to go even longer between feedings at night. Still, you usually shouldn't expect your baby to go all night without waking up for a feeding until he is four to six months old. Talk to your pediatrician if you think your baby is going too long at night without eating.

Also, six months is not a magic age at which all children stop needing to eat at night. Some older infants still need one or two feedings at night, although others aren't really hungry and are just used to eating to help them fall asleep. If you think that's the case, you can gradually decrease how many minutes your baby is breastfed at each nighttime feeding or put less formula in his bottle. You may have to go back to his customary feedings if he isn't satisfied with the decreased feedings or seems to wake up more afterward.

If your baby had been sleeping well at night and is now waking up more to eat, you should make sure that he is getting enough to eat during the day. This commonly happens when parents try to stretch their baby's daytime feedings past three or four hours. Adding an extra feeding back to your baby's daytime schedule will usually get him back to sleeping well again.

Part Six: All about Sleep

Even if you have a well-designed nursery and a beautiful crib, it can be tough to decide where your baby will sleep. Should you put her in her crib right away or use a bassinet or side sleeper to keep her close? Or do you plan on letting your baby sleep with you in your bed?

Your baby can start off in a crib, or you can first use a bassinet and then have her graduate to a crib once she outgrows her bassinet or is sleeping for longer stretches at a time. In the first few weeks and months, it can be easiest to keep your baby nearby in a bassinet, because she frequently wakes up to eat. That way, you can wake up, get her fed, and then put her right back to sleep. Even if your baby wakes up frequently, this can help everyone quickly get back to sleep and still get some rest through the night.

The main downside to having your baby nearby is that it may cause you to wake up every time that she stirs or wakes up briefly, even if it isn't a full awakening that requires your attention. That closeness does offer some reassurance, though, for many parents who worry about their younger baby through the night.

A bassinet is also a lot cozier than a crib will be for your newborn baby. On the other hand, starting her off in a crib does save you the expense of buying a bassinet, and if swaddled, she will likely feel just as cozy and comfortable in a crib.

In a 2005 SIDS Policy Statement, the AAP announced new guidelines about where infants should sleep—"A separate but proximate sleeping environment is recommended: The risk of SIDS has been shown to be reduced when the infant sleeps in the same room as the mother. A crib, bassinet, or cradle that conforms to the safety standards of the Consumer Product Safety Commission and ASTM (formerly the American Society for Testing and Materials) is recommended." In addition to figuring whether to use a crib or bassinet, parents of multiples also must decide if they want to let their babies sleep separately or together. Many opt to let their multiples sleep together in a bassinet or crib for at least their first few months and then separate them later on.

Don't Start Bad Habits

Since you have to decide what is best for your baby, you should avoid letting her get used to sleeping in a bouncy chair, moving swing, or car seat. Although all of these can be acceptable options, especially if it is hard to get your baby to sleep any other way, your baby may become dependent on them, and have a hard time moving to a crib later on.

Having your baby sleep in bed with you is a controversial way to put your baby to sleep. Although advocates praise the benefits of a family bed, other people question how safe it is and say that it may increase the risk of Sudden Infant Death Syndrome (SIDS). While the American Academy of Pediatrics and the Consumer Product Safety Commission are against co-sleeping, many other experts highly recommend the practice, including respected pediatrician and author William Sears, MD.

If you choose to share your bed with your baby, be sure to keep the bed safe, so that your baby can't roll off or get smothered by pillows and soft bedding and can't get trapped between the bed and a wall or headboard. Safer co-sleeping means using bedding that fits tightly on the mattress, avoiding pillows and soft blankets, and making sure that there is no room between the bed and the wall. A bedside sleeper or co-sleeper right next to your bed can be a safe way to get all of the benefits of having your baby sleep very close to you.

81 Look Forward to Sleeping Through the Night

Although you sometimes hear of some infants sleeping through the night at two months, the average infant doesn't begin to sleep all night until four to six months. It doesn't necessarily mean that you are doing something wrong if your younger infant isn't sleeping well or that other parents have a magic way to put their baby to sleep. Some babies are just naturally better sleepers than others.

If your baby isn't sleeping well by four to six months, or is waking up very frequently before that, you should look for things that may be interfering with your baby's sleep. Is he falling asleep while feeding or being rocked, then waking up every hour, and needing that same routine to get back to sleep? Then you may have created poor sleep associations and need to adjust your bedtime routine to help him fall asleep on his own.

Once your baby is two to three months old, you can begin to work on a regular bedtime routine to help him sleep through the night. That usually means putting him to sleep while he is drowsy, but still awake, so that he learns to fall asleep on his own. You can still get him ready for bed, perhaps give him a bath, read a story, or sing a lullaby. A last feeding will also be a part of his bedtime routine, but you should try to not let him fall asleep while eating as he gets older. Also, your baby will not learn to fall asleep on his own if he falls asleep watching a moving mobile or listening to music.

If your baby cries after you try putting him down while still awake, you should check on him after a few minutes and try to soothe him to sleep. The eventual goal will be for him to fall asleep without much fussing after you put him down.

The idea behind teaching your baby to fall asleep by himself is that if he later wakes up, then he will be able to simply put himself back to sleep. Everyone goes through brief periods of light sleep as they drift through different sleep stages. Infants who don't know how to go to sleep on their own often wake up during these light sleep stages, while those who do and have good sleep associations continue to sleep and are likely to sleep all night.

83 | Make Time for Naps

Because babies need a lot of sleep and they don't get all of their sleep at night, regular naps are an important part of their sleep schedule. In the first few weeks and months, as your baby is still in a regular sleeping, waking, and eating cycle, you don't have to think of daytime sleep as naps. They are just another part of your baby's overall need for sleep.

Later on, by three to four months, your baby's sleep will become more organized. You can then expect her to sleep more at night, and have three regular naps during the day. Although the length of naps varies, they are usually about one and a half hours each.

By six months, most infants only require two daytime naps, and they are sleeping even longer at night. This routine of an early morning and early afternoon nap will probably continue until your child is well into his toddler years. If your baby doesn't nap well, make sure that you are not waiting until she is overtired before putting her down, and that you have a regular and strict routine for naps. Your infant is less likely to take good naps if she sometimes takes a nap at home, sometimes in the car, and falls asleep in her stroller other times. Try to organize your daytime schedule around your baby's naps. In general, regular long naps are much better than more frequent, short naps.

In addition to frequently waking up, common sleep problems include having trouble falling asleep and simply not sleeping enough. They all can contribute to both you and your baby not getting enough sleep, leading to fussy and irritable babies and parents. The most common sleep problems include:

- Taking a long time to fall asleep
- Frequently waking up
- Waking up too early in the morning
- Not taking regular, long naps during the day
- Having a backward sleep schedule, sleeping a lot during the day and staying up most of the night

Most of these problems can be resolved by avoiding the bad habits mentioned earlier, sticking to a regular routine for naps and bedtime, and teaching your infant to fall asleep on her own with a good bedtime routine.

Swaddling in a blanket is a popular way to help babies sleep well. Being wrapped firmly in a blanket can help to prevent him from making jerking movements that can wake him up and will help him to sleep cozy and secure. You should stop swaddling your baby as he gets older, especially once he is able to roll over.

Avoid Common Sleep Mistakes

Many sleep problems can be avoided if you have real-istic expectations and know the bad habits to avoid. The following are some pieces of advice to help you avoid some of the most common sleep mistakes and misunderstandings:

- Don't let your newborn skip meals because he is sleeping a lot. Although you don't have to wake up an older baby who is feeding and gaining weight well, in the first few weeks you should wake your baby up if he has gone more than four to six hours without eating.
- Don't start solid foods such as cereal early to help your baby sleep longer.
- Don't wait until your baby is overtired to put him to sleep.
- Be careful not to skip naps because you are out and about and busy. Try to adjust your daily rou-tine to your child's nap schedule.
- Don't put your younger infant to sleep with a security object, such as a large stuffed animal or blanket, because it may raise the risk of SIDS.

One of the most important sleep habits to avoid is putting your baby to sleep on his stomach, even if you think it helps him to sleep better. The extra risk of SIDS isn't worth a little more sleep at night.

Before you even begin to look for advice on fixing a sleep problem, you first have to decide whether you or your baby even has a problem. If your nine- or twelve-month-old is sleeping for four or five hours at a time, wakes up once or twice at night to feed, and you both quickly go back to sleep, then there may not really be a problem. Especially if everyone is well rested the next day, you may not want to adjust anything to eliminate those feedings or awakenings.

How about if your older infant continues to fall asleep breastfeeding or with a bottle or pacifier? Isn't that a problem? It can be if she hasn't learned to fall asleep on her own and is frequently waking up after falling asleep like that. However, if your bedtime routine works for you and your baby is sleeping well, then it isn't really a problem that needs to be fixed.

Consider Expert Advice

The Happiest Baby on the Block is without a doubt one of the most popular books about crying babies. Its author, Harvey Karp, MD, offers a "new way to calm crying and help your newborn baby sleep longer." Part of the book's popularity is that it offers specific and easy-to-try techniques that soothe and calm many babies.

Most of those techniques, summarized by the "five S's," are things that everyone tries almost instinctively and understands. Most parents try to **swaddle** their baby, let them **suck** on a pacifier, **swing** them or use rhythmic motions, and use a "**shhhing**" **sound** to comfort their baby. Some even discover that **side-lying** (holding your baby so that his right or left side is up, facing away from you) is helpful. But when these techniques aren't working for you, Dr. Karp offers tips for using them in the right way and in the right order. If you don't want to read the whole book or still find Dr. Karp's techniques hard to understand, video and DVD versions are also available so that you can directly see his methods.

Although most parents who try the five S's like them, one common complaint is that some babies get "spoiled" and become dependent on swaddling to get to sleep. Parents then have a new problem when they later have to wean their baby from swaddling and get him to sleep on his own.

It can be hard to live in a sleep-deprived state for much of your infant's first few months. Not only do you have less energy for your baby and your other children, but you may also have trouble keeping up at work and in your other responsibilities. This is a situation in which you should absolutely get help. In addition to Mom and Dad taking turns caring for the baby at night, you can also consider hiring a night nanny. Although not inexpensive, they can provide total care overnight or simply bring your baby to Mom for breastfeedings, allowing parents to get a good night's rest. Or maybe you could ask a family member to stay overnight and to pitch in for free.

Sing to Your Baby

An old-fashioned lullaby can be a fun way to play with and bond with your baby, as well as help her calm down and relax for sleep. Knowing a few lullabies, such as Brahms's "Lullaby," "Rock-a-Bye Baby," and "Hush, Little Baby," can help you feel more comfortable singing to your baby.

Don't worry if you don't remember all of the words. Your baby won't mind. The sound of your voice and expressions on your face are often more important than the actual lyrics. You can simply make up your own words to finish the lullaby. Or you could also sing any of your favorite songs in a lullaby type of tone. Or just make up your own lullabies. As long as some of the words rhyme, your baby will likely love it.

As in all other aspects of parenting, a father should have an equal role with his partner when it comes to caring for his baby at night. This usually means taking turns attending to the baby each night or each time he wakes up. That way, both parents can get some sleep, especially during the first few months when nighttime awakenings are the most common.

A father can help with nighttime feedings even if his baby is exclusively breastfed. He can feed a bottle of pumped breastmilk or even simply bring the baby to Mom to breastfeed and then return the baby to the bassinet or crib.

If you decide that one parent will take on the sole role of caring for the baby at night, then the other can make up for it by doing more at other times. This is a good compromise if, for example, one parent has a very hard time getting back to sleep after waking up at night. Good ways to make up for not getting up in the middle of the night can include taking over the first and last feedings of the day, so that your partner can go to sleep a little earlier and sleep in the next morning.

Part Seven

Is This Normal?

New parents always try to do what's best for their baby. Unfortunately, they can sometimes misunderstand many of the normal things that babies do, thinking that those things are a problem. This can lead to unnecessary treatments, dietary changes, and worry, which themselves can cause something that is normal to become a real problem. Reviewing these normal things that babies do can help you to keep with the basic principle of "do no harm," just as your pediatrician does.

Understand That Colic Is Common

Crying babies often just get labeled as having colic or being colicky. Colic is usually defined as a daily period of crying for one to three hours in the early evening, although it may occur at other times or even throughout the day, in an otherwise healthy baby. After starting at about two to three weeks of age, it usually reaches its peak at six weeks and then gradually improves over the next month or two.

Colic is very common, but nobody really knows what causes it. The many theories about it include the possibility that these babies have immature nervous systems or immature gastrointestinal systems. Other people believe that babies with colic have food sensitivities, are simply overstimulated and cry to let off steam, or have anxious parents.

While the cause isn't known, it is well accepted that colicky babies usually outgrow their crying by about three months of age. Because there are other medical causes of crying, you shouldn't just dismiss your baby's crying as colic. If you do, a serious medical problem might be overlooked. At the same time, you don't want to put your baby through unnecessary tests or treatments. By the time you get through three or four formula changes, two or three medicines for reflux, and an upper GI, your baby with colic will probably already have reached his peak time of crying and will be getting better on his own.

Most babies normally spit up at least some of the time. It may be when they eat a little too much, don't burp well, or get too excited after a meal. Other babies spit up after most or all of their feedings. Aside from cleaning up the messes, there usually is nothing to worry about. Signs that your baby's spitting up is a problem can include that he is fussy for most of the day or night, seems to be choking or having trouble breathing when he spits up, or isn't gaining weight well.

For normal spitting up, you often don't have to do anything except keep burp rags handy to minimize messes. Changing your baby's formula isn't usually helpful, although thickened formulas sometimes decrease the amount of spitting up. Other nonmedical interventions might include feeding your baby smaller amounts more frequently if the spitting up seems to be related to the amount he drinks at one time, or burping your baby more often during each feeding. You might also hold your baby upright after feedings and try to reduce how much stimulation he gets after his feedings.

Many babies stop spitting up around six to nine months old, or once they are sitting up well and eating more solid foods. Other babies don't stop until much later, when they are twelve to eighteen months old. Talk to your pediatrician if your baby's reflux (spitting up) isn't getting better over time, or begins causing problems.

Part Seven: Is This Normal?

Deal with Hiccups and Gas

Hiccups and gas are other normal things that parents worry about and often overtreat. Neither usually requires any treatment or change in diet at all. Hiccups are hardly ever a sign of a problem, although gas can be if it is associated with other symptoms, such as diarrhea or excessive crying.

The big problem occurs when you have a baby who cries a lot while having hiccups or gas. Is your baby just swallowing a lot of air when he is crying, which causes hiccups and gas? Or is he crying *because* of the hiccups and gas? In situations like this, seeing your pediatrician is usually best to try to sort things out. You should avoid giving your baby a lot of gas drops or making dietary changes on your own, because they are often unnecessary.

A baby's bowel movements change so much during her first year. They go from the thick, black, tarry meconium stools of the first few days to the yellow, seedy, breastmilk stools. Formula-fed babies' stools will change too, and they will usually be a little firmer than breastfed babies.

How often your baby has bowel movements will also change over time. For younger infants, especially in their first few weeks of life, not having regular bowel movements can be a sign of a serious problem. Especially for breastfed babies, constipation may indicate that your baby isn't getting enough to eat. By two to three months, some breastfed babies might only have a bowel movement once a week. Even formula-fed babies might not have bowel movements every day. Keep in mind that if your baby has true constipation, in addition to having infrequent stools, the ones that she does have will be large and firm or small hard balls. If they are soft, then your baby likely isn't really constipated.

Your baby's stools might also change in response to new foods that you introduce into her diet. This commonly occurs when you start a baby on cereal for the first time, or change her formula. Start new foods slowly so you can easily identify which food is causing the problem. Even if you aren't giving new foods to your baby directly, breastfed babies can react to foods in their mother's diet and have changes in their bowel movements.

Recognizing the many normal changes that your baby's bowel movements might have is important. If you think every green or loose stool is a problem, then you might make unnecessary changes to her diet or eliminate important foods. If your baby's stools are worrying you, talk to your pediatrician before you change formulas or make any other changes.

No matter how big or small a baby is at birth, most dads expect that he will quickly grow into a big, bouncing, bundle of joy. But how big will he get? And how quickly will he get there? Although growth patterns vary from child to child, you can expect that your infant will:

- Regain his birth weight by two weeks and then gain 1½ to 2 pounds a month
- Gain about 1 pound a month beginning at three months
- Double his birth weight by five months
- Triple his birth weight by twelve months
- Grow about 10 inches in his first year, although he won't double his birth height until he is three to four years old

You can expect that a baby's head will grow about four inches in his first year. However, keep in mind that your baby may grow a little slower or faster than these averages. Your baby's weight at birth and his very early growth both usually represent conditions during your partner's pregnancy. After a few months, genetics often take over. At this time, a big baby born to small parents will often slow down in his growth, while a small baby born to big parents might grow more quickly and move up on his growth charts.

Part Seven: Is This Normal?

Understand Growth Charts and Percentiles

An important part of your baby's well-child visits to his pediatrician is recording his height, weight, and head circumference on a growth chart. It's common for parents to get confused trying to understand these growth charts. Keep in mind that the 50th percentile represents the average child. But whether children are above or below the 50th percentile does not indicate how well or poorly they are growing. By definition, one-half of kids are below that percentile, and one-half are above it. So kids at the 5th, 25th, and 95th percentile can all be growing normally. What do those numbers mean then? Well, a child at the 5th percentile is bigger than 5 percent of kids at the same age. Likewise, a child at the 95th percentile is bigger than 95 percent of kids.

Parents are often more concerned about percentiles than pediatricians are. Because the percentile doesn't really indicate whether a child is growing normally, pediatricians look more to the fact that a child is staying at the same percentile or growth curve. Steady growth along a growth curve is usually the best indication that a child is growing normally.

In addition to how well their baby is growing, parents often are concerned about her development. Is your baby meeting her developmental milestones on time? Is she rolling over and sitting up when she should? Is she keeping up with other kids that you know who are the same age? Of course, you should talk to your pediatrician if you think your baby isn't developing on time. Some warning signs about your child's development to look for include that she:

- Seems to have a hand preference early on
- Is delayed on many or all of her milestones and doesn't seem to be catching up
- Doesn't look at you or follow things by six weeks, which can be a sign of blindness
- Doesn't startle at loud noises, which can be a sign of a hearing loss
- Seems floppy or has poor muscle tone
- Seems rigid, with increased muscle tone

If you are concerned that your baby hasn't reached a milestone, well-child visits are a good time to talk about this and also for your pediatrician to observe which milestones your baby has reached since the last visit. In considering your child's development, your pediatrician probably will ask about her social or personal development, language, and fine and gross motor skills.

Part Seven: Is This Normal?

Watch for Blocked Tear Ducts

Tears drain from the inner corner of the eye to the nose through the nasolacrimal ducts. In some infants, this duct is blocked, so tears can't drain to the nose. Instead, the eye tears a lot. Other symptoms can include some redness around the eye and a yellowish discharge from the affected eye.

In most cases, the tear duct will open up on its own by the time your baby is a year old. This can be helped by massaging the side of the nose where the tear duct is. If the tear duct doesn't eventually open up on its own, or if your child's tear duct gets frequently infected, then your pediatrician can use a probe to open it up.

Cradle cap is often more distressing for parents than for the babies who have it. The thick, yellow scale or flaky, dry skin that accompanies cradle cap doesn't look normal, but it usually is not as bad as it looks. Most babies don't develop any symptoms, the cradle cap doesn't bother them, and it eventually goes away on its own.

If it does bother you or your child, though, you can treat it. The most common treatment involves simply massaging baby oil into the affected areas and then using a soft brush to loosen and remove the scales. More persistent cases might respond to a medicated shampoo, such as Selsun Blue or Nizoral A-D, used a few times a week. Talk to your pediatrician if the rash seems very itchy or if your baby also has an itchy rash all over the rest of his body.

Don't Worry about Hair Loss

Different types of hair loss, or alopecia, can affect your baby. One of the most common is traction alopecia, which results from the back of your baby's head rubbing against surfaces he lies on. The hair in this area will eventually grow back once your baby is sitting up more and rolling over.

Another type of normal hair loss that affects infants is called telogen effluvium, and involves the process by which baby hairs fall out. These hairs are eventually replaced by mature hairs after a few months.

When an infant has an umbilical hernia, his belly button will protrude out at times. It often becomes worse when he strains or cries, and then goes back in if you push on it or when he relaxes. Although impressive looking, especially when they are large, umbilical hernias almost always go away on their own, though sometimes not until your child is four or five years old.

Folk remedies, such as taping a coin to hold the hernia in, aren't helpful and should be avoided. If the hernia is very large or isn't improving at all over time, surgical correction might be done earlier than age five years. You should also call your pediatrician if the hernia seems stuck out or is painful.

Consider the Pros and Cons of Pacifiers and Thumb Sucking

Using a pacifier or sucking on her thumb or fingers isn't necessarily a bad habit for a baby. Many younger infants actually enjoy the security they get from this type of non-nutritive sucking, and it can be something that is healthy and normal and encouraged. It also can provide a calming or soothing effect for many infants. The problem lies more with prolonged thumb-sucking or pacifier use. If a child continues to use a pacifier or suck her thumb past age three to five years, then it can affect her teeth and speech and language development.

Fortunately, most infants give up these habits well before they become a problem, often by age six to nine months. To help keep this healthy habit from turning into a bad habit, you might try one of the following strategies:

- Avoid the types of pacifiers that clip on your baby's clothes, which makes it always available.
- Get your older infant attached to another type of security object, such as a small blanket.
- Don't be so quick to put the pacifier back in her mouth each time it comes out.

The most frequent cause of a runny nose in younger kids is the common cold. Like most other viral infections, there is no treatment for the common cold, and you often just have to treat your child's symptoms until he gets over them on his own.

These symptoms typically begin with a clear runny nose, low-grade fever, and a cough. Over the next few days the symptoms may worsen, with a higher fever and worsening cough. The runny nose might become yellow or green before going away over the next one to two weeks. It is important to understand that this is the normal pattern for a cold, and it does not mean that your child has a sinus infection or needs antibiotics. Of course, if your child is very fussy, is not eating or drinking, or has trouble breathing, then a trip to your doctor is a good idea.

While a yellow or green runny nose is typically caused by a common cold, if the infection lingers for more than ten to fourteen days and is worsening, or if the child has a high fever for more than three or four days and appears ill, then he may really have a sinus infection that requires antibiotics.

Part Seven: Is This Normal?

Look Out for Ear Infections

Parents often suspect that their child has an ear infection when he starts pulling on his ears, but unless there are other symptoms, such as a fever or irritability, the ears are usually normal.

More typically, an ear infection will develop a few days or weeks after having a cold. A child will experience ear pain, irritability, fever, and a decreased appetite when he gets an ear infection. Although symptoms sometimes go away without treatment, doctors still commonly prescribe antibiotics, especially for children under the age of twelve to twenty-four months.

An ear infection shouldn't be confused with simply having fluid in the middle ear, which commonly occurs after an ear infection. This fluid doesn't usually require treatment and will often go away in two to three months. If it isn't going away, a child may need treatment with ear tubes, especially if it is causing a hearing loss. Frequent or persistent infections can also be a sign that your child needs ear tubes.

A diaper rash is one of the more common rashes that your baby might have during his first year. It is often caused by irritation and can be prevented with frequent diaper changes and use of a barrier-type diaper rash medication, such as A+D, Balmex, or Desitin. Various diaper rash creams and ointments also can be used to treat most diaper rashes. If the rash doesn't go away, especially if it is bright red and surrounded by small red bumps, then it may be caused by a yeast infection. You should use an over-the-counter or prescription strength antifungal cream in addition to a diaper rash medication to clear up this type of secondary infection.

Part Eight

Safety First

Babyproofing the house before your baby first comes home is fairly easy because newborn babies and even younger infants aren't very mobile and can't get into too much trouble. But once your baby starts crawling and walking, you have to be much more careful. In fact, you may have to begin babyproofing again, so your child isn't hurt in an avoidable injury or accident.

Avoid Car Seat Mistakes

Even with all of the publicity about car seat safety, the detailed instructions included with each car seat, and the car seat safety checkups provided in most communities, people continue to make mistakes in how they put their kids in their car seat. Among the more common mistakes are:

- Putting the harness chest clip in the wrong position and not at armpit level
- Allowing the harness straps to become loose, twisted, or positioned too high above the infant's shoulders
- Placing a child in a forward-facing seat before he is twenty pounds and twelve months old
- Placing a child in a rear-facing car seat in the path of an air bag
- Putting a blanket or heavy jacket under the harness straps

Be sure you avoid these mistakes. You should also read the instructions when you install your child's car seat. If you still aren't sure that you are using it correctly, go to a car seat safety inspection station. You can find one in your area at the website *www.seatcheck.org*.

It is never too soon to childproof your house, but do it at least before your baby is six months old. If you wait much longer, your infant may already be crawling, cruising, or walking, and you probably then won't discover hazards until they have already hurt your child.

Although the kitchen and the bathroom can be especially hazardous, every room of the house that your baby can enter has to be safe. There are many basic safety measures to take care of in each room, including:

- Putting covers on unused electrical outlets (These can range from simple plastic plugs to more sophisticated covers that slide or pop off to make outlets easily accessible.)
- Installing gates on stairs, both at the top and bottom of each staircase
- Either removing furniture with sharp edges or installing soft guards
- Removing breakables from low shelves and tables
- Placing nonskid backing on rugs that your child might slip or slide on
- Installing "no-tip" accessories or wall anchors for heavy furniture so it can't fall over on your child

Part Eight: Safety First

- Placing finger guards on doors so they don't slam on your infant's fingers
- Keeping cords for window shades or blinds out of reach
- Placing window guards on upstairs windows so your kids won't fall through the screens if the window is open
- Securing electrical cords with cord holders and electrical outlet protectors/plastic plug
- Setting the temperature of hot water heaters to 120° Fahrenheit

You should also look carefully for hidden dangers and remove them. Things to watch for range from the little plastic caps on door stops, which kids can choke on, to heavy items on low carts or tables that can easily tip over, especially TVs.

One of the biggest dangers in the kitchen is the stove. There are now many devices to make the stove safe, including locks for the knobs and adjustable covers or guards to keep your baby away from things cooking on the stovetop. You should also secure your other kitchen appliances. Even the dishwasher and refrigerator can be hazards, so place a locking strap on each to keep your kids out.

Kitchen cabinets are often harder to secure than you would think, and they contain many things that could be hazardous to a young child. There are many safety products to help childproof your cabinets. You can choose either a system that latches on to the outside of cabinet handles, which is simpler to install but easy to forget to put back on, or one that installs inside the cabinet as a latch. Or use a combination of the two, especially on the cabinets that contain cleaners, poisons, or breakables.

As in the kitchen, you should secure the drawers and cabinets in your bathroom. Also consider installing toilet lid locks to prevent drowning, and keep hot appliances such as curling irons out of your infant's reach. A nonslip mat and a faucet cushion can help make the bathtub safe, too.

Part Eight: Safety First

Childproof the Fireplace

While a warm fire is nice on a cold night, fireplaces are hard to keep childproofed. Among the dangers are the sharp edges around the hearth and the risk of getting burned when you have a fire going.

The easiest way to childproof a fireplace is to simply place a heat-resistant safety gate around the whole thing. That way you don't have to worry about your kids getting into the fireplace and playing with ashes, falling on the sharp corners of the hearth, or getting close to the flames. If your fireplace is fueled by natural gas, be sure to secure your gas key, place a cover on your gas valve cover, and install a carbon monoxide detector.

If you do a good job of childproofing your house, your infant shouldn't be at too much risk of getting into any real poisons. If he does get into a poison, such as one of your own medicines, household cleaners, or something even more serious such as a pesticide, do you know what to do?

The American Academy of Pediatrics no longer recommends that parents keep syrup of ipecac in their homes to induce vomiting. Instead, you should just call Poison Control. This used to mean remembering your local poison control number, but getting help got a lot easier several years ago when the system was switched to a single nationwide toll-free number. To call your nearest poison control center from anywhere in the United States, you now simply dial 1-800-222-1222, and a poison safety expert will help you figure out what to do for your child.

To prevent poisonings, remember to use products with child-resistant caps, even vitamins and herbal supplements. Store your household cleaners, chemicals, and insecticides out of reach in inaccessible, locked cabinets. Also keep all hazardous products in their original containers, instead of transferring them to a milk or soda bottle to use them.

Rethink Mobile Baby Walkers

Mobile baby walkers are one product for infants that have always had a bad reputation. If you are considering buying or using a mobile baby walker, keep in mind that the American Academy of Pediatrics has actually called for a ban on their sale because they are associated with so many injuries, and they won't help your baby learn to walk any faster. Why are mobile baby walkers so unsafe?

Well, they aren't. The problem with mobile baby walkers is that they make your baby mobile. And often they make your baby too mobile, allowing her to get into things that aren't safe. Still, if your house is well childproofed and your child is well supervised and kept away from stairs or other dangers, a mobile baby walker can be safe and fun for your baby to use.

An alternative to a mobile baby walker can be a stationary walker or activity center. These include lots of bells and whistles to keep your older infant entertained.

Parents often worry about their baby choking on food once he starts finger and table foods, but the average house has a lot of other choking hazards that put infants even more at risk. These hazards can range from large pieces of food to coins your baby may find on the floor to your older children's toys. The following tips can help keep your baby safe from choking:

- Once your infant is eight to nine months old and you start offering finger foods, cut them up into small, bite-size pieces.
- Avoid giving "choke foods," such as grapes, peanuts, and chewing gum, to your infant or toddler.
- Only let your infant play with age-appropriate toys (no parts smaller than 1¼ inch in diameter and 2½ inches long).
- If you have older kids, consider putting their toys, which often do have small parts, in a separate room that your infant can't enter.
- Warn older children not to give their younger siblings foods or toys that they might choke on.
- Let your younger infant play with Mylar balloons instead of rubber or latex balloons, which can be a choking hazard if they pop.
- Look for and pick up small objects, such as coins, pins, batteries, and buttons, each time you put your baby down on the floor.

First aid for a choking infant usually involves placing the child face down on your lap and giving five back blows with the heel of your hand to the area just between the infant's shoulder blades. If that doesn't work, the next step is placing the infant face up and giving five compressions to the infant's breastbone. A CPR class can teach you more first aid to help a choking infant.

The American Heart Association recommends using the Heimlich Maneuver, a series of under-the-diaphragm abdominal thrusts, for children older than age one.

Although it seems that most child products, household products, and toys are being built to high safety standards, each year many children are hurt or killed by unsafe products that have already been recalled. Do you know whether any of the products in your home have been recalled?

Unfortunately, it is often up to parents to identify which products have been recalled, and then either repair these unsafe products or remove them from their homes. Even if you send in your product registration card, there is no guarantee that you will be notified if the product has been recalled, so regularly watch the news, magazines, and websites for recall alerts and information. Also visit the website *www.recalls. gov*, which makes it easy to find all types of recalled products, including consumer products, motor vehicles (including cars and car seats), boats, food, medicine, cosmetics, and environmental products.

Even more of a concern is the rise in popularity of buying used products, some of which may have been recalled, from online auction sites. As long as you check to be sure a product hasn't been recalled, most used baby accessories can be safe. However, don't buy a used car seat on the Internet, because there is no way to make sure that it wasn't damaged in a car crash.

Part Eight: Safety First

Use Sunscreen on Your Baby

Keeping your kids safe from the harmful effects of the sun is very important. Most people get 80 percent of their lifetime exposure to the sun before age eighteen. Increased exposure means increased risk of skin cancer, so it is never too soon to start limiting that exposure.

In addition to using sunscreen, sun safety can include keeping your child covered up with light, loose-fitting clothing, a hat, and sunglasses. It's also best to avoid being outdoors during the hottest part of the day, between about 10 A.M. and 4 P.M.

Younger children often are forgotten when the family puts on sunscreen, because the parents think it isn't necessary or just not appropriate for infants. Although the American Academy of Pediatrics (AAP) used to recommend using sunscreen on infants only after six months old, they recently revised their guidelines. Now the AAP says that parents can apply a minimal amount of sunscreen with at least 15 SPF (sun protection factor) to small areas such as the infant's face and the back of the hands even to babies younger than six months.

Apply sunscreen at least thirty minutes before going outside, and use sunscreen even on cloudy days. You should then reapply sunscreen about every two hours, or sooner if your child was in the water.

Insect bites used to be considered a simple nuisance. The biggest problem they caused was an itchy, or sometimes painful, red spot. The rise in West Nile disease and other insect-borne illnesses makes it even more important to keep your children safe from insects.

The most commonly used insect repellents are made with DEET, which can be safely used on infants as young as two months of age. Although you shouldn't put the insect repellent on your infant's hands or around her mouth or eyes, you can put it on other exposed areas of skin or clothing. Always be sure to wash it off once you get back inside.

Alternatives to DEET include natural insect repellents, including those that contain citronella or soybean oil. They may not work as well as insect repellents with DEET, but they are a good alternative if you aren't convinced that DEET is safe to use on younger children.

Remember Pool and Water Safety

Drowning is a leading cause of death for younger children, so it is important to keep your backyard pool safe. Even if your young children know how to swim, they should not be considered drown-proof and should always be supervised around the water. In addition to not leaving your children alone around a pool, you can keep your kids safe by:

- Putting a fence around your pool with a self-closing and self-latching gate
- Locking or childproofing all exits from your house that lead to the pool
- Leaving a telephone by the pool so that you can quickly call for help if you need it
- Keeping toys away from the sides of the pool so that you don't attract younger children, who might fall in
- Storing rescue equipment near the pool so you are ready in an emergency

But pools aren't the only drowning risk for younger children. A crawling baby can pull up on a bucket, fall in, and quickly drown. Other hazards include the bathtub, toilet, and any other container of water. Remember to never leave your infant alone near any water, not even for just a few seconds, which is more than enough time for your baby to drown.

Having a family pet is a popular tradition in many families. For your infant's safety, remember that no matter how kid-safe that you think your dog or cat is, you should never leave your baby unsupervised around an animal. Any pet, even one that is usually tame and playful, can bite or attack if it feels threatened by an aggressive infant who is pulling on its ears or invading its space.

Some families also enjoy having more exotic pets, such as iguanas, turtles, snakes, and other reptiles. Because of the risk of salmonella to children who touch or handle these reptiles, which can cause fever, vomiting, and diarrhea, younger children shouldn't have any contact with these types of reptiles. You should even be careful to wash your hands and any surfaces that touch the reptile with soap and water so that you don't contaminate your younger children. Small baby turtles with shells less than four inches in length are especially dangerous, because younger kids can put them in their mouths. In fact, sales of such turtles has been banned by the FDA.

Part Eight: Safety First

Prepare for a Fire

Every floor or level of your house should have a working smoke alarm. They are especially important inside or just outside each and every bedroom. To prevent false or nuisance alarms, don't install a smoke alarm inside the kitchen or bathrooms. The manufacturer's instructions and your local building and safety codes can also help you find the best places in your home for smoke alarms. To make sure that your smoke alarms are in good working condition, change the batteries at least once a year and test the alarms each month.

Make a Fire Escape Plan

No matter how safe your home is and how many smoke alarms you have, if you don't have a plan for everyone to get out of the house, your family may still not be safe in case of a fire. A well-planned and regularly practiced fire escape plan can help to make sure that everyone gets out safely. As part of your fire escape plan, you should decide who will get each of your children out of the house, how they will get out, a backup route in case the first is blocked or unusable, and where you will meet outside. This way you won't have to worry about anyone rushing back into the house trying to reach a child who is already out safely.

Most people understand the need for having smoke alarms in their home, but carbon monoxide detectors are often overlooked, even though the Consumer Product Safety Commission recommends that every home have one. Carbon monoxide detectors are especially important if you have a garage attached to your home or if you have any fuel burning, nonelectric appliances in your home. These can include:

- Furnaces
- Fireplaces
- Stoves
- Water heaters
- Space heaters

In addition to having these types of appliances professionally inspected each year and providing them with adequate ventilation, you should have carbon monoxide alarms to help alert you to any leaks before they can poison your family. Like smoke alarms, they should be installed near your bedrooms and on every floor of your house.

The biggest exposures to lead these days is from lead paint in older homes, especially those built before 1950 and homes built before 1978 that are being remodeled, and soil that is contaminated with lead. If your house was built during the time when lead-based paint was still used, keep a close eye out for peeling, chipping paint that your baby might try to eat. Also watch for lead in your drinking water or on your clothes.

Drinking Water and Lead

Lead may also be used in pipes, which means that drinking water is likely to be the biggest source of exposure to lead for your baby. Although only homes built before 1930 are likely to have lead pipes, the pipes in newer homes may have been connected with lead solder. And keep in mind that even "lead-free" pipes can be made with up to 8 percent lead.

If your plumbing might have lead in it, be sure to only use cold water from the tap to make formula or for cooking and drinking, because hot water can have higher lead levels than cold water. You should also let the water run for fifteen to thirty seconds before using it, to help flush your pipes so that the water has less lead in it. A water filter might also help to reduce the amount of lead in your drinking water.

Other Sources of Lead

Lead is still used today in many products, including batteries and solder, which means that if you work in certain industries you may present a potential risk to your children because lead dust can get on your clothes. Among the jobs and hobbies that can be a risk to your family are:

- Auto repair
- Welding
- Construction
- Radiator repair
- Battery repair
- Making pottery
- Making stained glass

If you spend time doing any of these activities, you should wash and change your clothes and shoes before leaving your place of work or entering your home. Washing your work clothes separately from the rest of the family's clothes is also a good idea to keep them from getting contaminated.

Part Nine

Parenting Economics

The economics of raising a new baby is going to mean different things for each family. A father with a lot of credit card debt who is living paycheck to paycheck is going to have different needs and priorities than a father who is more well-off and is already planning his baby's college fund. Although family finances can be a stressful topic, thinking about them is important, no matter what your situation.

Decide on One Income or Two

The decision about whether or not both parents should work after they begin having kids is a lot more complicated than most people realize. There isn't just the extra income to consider. You also have to consider many other pros and cons, including commuting expenses; benefits received in addition to income, such as insurance or a 401(k) plan; the cost of day care; and the amount of taxes you pay on that income.

For people who have free, familiar day care, such as a grandparent or other family member who can watch the baby during the day, or for parents who are both very committed to their careers, choosing to continue in a two-income lifestyle may be a very easy decision.

Likewise, if a family plans to have one parent stay home, and one parent makes much more money than the other and has better benefits or a stronger future at the job, they also will have an easy decision to make. But it becomes harder to make this decision when you're not sure how to downsize your spending to fit one income, or when one parent makes much less money but is the only source of health insurance or a company retirement plan. Consider using a day-care cost calculator on the Internet or talking to a financial advisor if you are having a hard time deciding whether it makes more economic sense for both parents to work or for one to stay home.

When one parent stays home, it is often the mom. Although often viewed as a "dream job," staying at home can be hard for many new mothers. In addition to the sometimes unappreciated work of caring for their kids and their home, the lack of contact and communication with other adults can be too much for some mothers. A helpful dad and a good support system can make it easier for a stay-at-home mom who is struggling.

The traditional roles of a career dad and stay-at-home mom also are sometimes reversed. More and more dads are staying home and caring for their kids while Mom goes to work. Sometimes this continues until the children are grown, while other times Mom and Dad take turns staying home for a few years at a time.

There are many reasons why dads will stay home. Sometimes it is out of necessity, when Dad loses a job and can't find work. Or maybe Mom has a much higher paying job and it makes more sense for her to be the "breadwinner." But often, the reason is simply that Dad wants to stay home, care for his kids, and have more time to spend with them. As more and more dads stay home with their kids, this should be viewed as a good option for families who don't want to put their kids in day care or hire a nanny.

Part Nine: Parenting Economics

Depending on how large a company you work for, you may be entitled to up to twelve weeks of leave when you have or adopt a new baby. This paternity leave is mandated by the Family and Medical Leave Act (FMLA), but it has many restrictions and mainly applies to people who work in government jobs or for larger employers. If you work for a company that has fewer than fifty employees, you may not be entitled to paternity leave at all.

Unfortunately, even when you do qualify for paternity leave, that time off will likely be unpaid. Can you afford to take three months off of work? If not, consider taking just one or two weeks of leave or use some paid vacation time instead. If you plan for it in advance, you may be able to take more time off when your baby is born. This might mean saving up sick days and vacation time, or working extra before the baby is born and saving up some money to get you through your paternity leave.

Staying home and caring for a baby is a full-time job in itself for most parents. That makes it hard to understand how anyone could stay home, care for the baby, plus have another job on the side. Especially in the first few months and years, when your baby is going to demand a lot of your time, working at home can be difficult.

However, some people have been known to make this work for them. For example, working at home may be an option if you have a very flexible, part-time work-at-home job and you have extra help around the house. Be sure to carefully consider the demands of this option before deciding whether you or your partner can make this kind of commitment to an employer. Be realistic with yourself about what the job requires, and whether it will be possible to meet those demands as well as the needs of your infant.

125 Try Working Opposite Shifts

Another way to avoid day care or a nanny, even when both parents are working, is for parents to have opposite work shifts. With this type of arrangement, one parent may work at night, while the other works during the day. Or one parent may just work a few shifts on the weekend, when the other parent has time off.

Having different work schedules allows one parent to always be home with the child, but it can put a big strain on the rest of family life. Because one parent will likely be coming home as the other is leaving for work, it doesn't give the couple much quality time together.

That big drawback makes this type of arrangement most useful for families in which the parents already were working in opposite shifts when they had their baby. Maybe one parent has a traditional daytime office job, while the other works the night shift as a nurse, police officer, or in tech support. These new parents are probably already used to their arrangement. It may not be as good an idea for parents who look to move to opposite shifts after they have their baby.

If you decide that both parents are going to go to work each day, next you will have to decide who is going to take care of your baby. This decision will be easy if you have a trusted family member who is willing to babysit each day. If this isn't an option for you, the usual choices are enrolling your baby in a group or home day care or hiring a nanny to watch your baby in your house.

Each option has it own pros and cons, so be prepared to do some research. For example, a nanny is the most expensive option, and it means trusting one person to be alone with your child, but your child will be around fewer kids and will be less likely to get sick often. A group day care will expose your child to a lot of other kids (and their germs). While he might get sick a little more often in a group day care, these facilities are also often thought of as being the most well supervised, as there are many other people around and your child isn't usually alone with just one caregiver. Check out the options in your area carefully, and don't hesitate to ask plenty of questions before signing up anyone's services.

Part Nine: Parenting Economics

Get Health Insurance

The need to have health insurance is one of the easier financial topics for most parents to understand. Even regular visits to your pediatrician can be expensive, but if your child develops medical problems or ends up being hospitalized, the expenses can quickly add up and cripple a family financially.

Choosing a Plan

In general, indemnity plans, which allow you to see whichever doctor you want and send the bill to your insurance company, will provide many more choices than managed care plans, such as Preferred Provider Organizations (PPOs) and Health Maintenance Organizations (HMOs). However, indemnity plans are likely to be much more expensive than managed care plans. Here are some other things to consider when choosing insurance that will cover your new child:

- If possible, choose a PPO or POS (Point of Service) plan. These plans usually offer more choices and more independence, such as seeing specialists without a referral. If you choose an HMO, make sure that there are pediatric specialists on the plan.
- Make sure that vaccines are a covered expense, especially during your baby's first year, because he will be getting shots at most visits.

- Consider getting prescription drug coverage. Most antibiotics and other medications can easily cost $40 to $100 each and may be more than the doctor's visit costs.
- If there is a children's hospital in your area, make sure that it is on the health insurance plan that you choose.
- Try to get insurance through a group health plan if your baby or any other family members have a chronic illness that might count as a pre-existing condition. With an individual plan, that condition likely won't be covered for at least a year.

You should also consider what your copays and deductibles are. Choosing a health insurance plan that costs $100 less per month doesn't make sense if you are going to be paying $1,500 or $2,000 extra each year in copays and deductibles. In the end, you will have to balance the cost of the insurance plan with your own needs.

Look into Other Kinds of Insurance

Once you become a father, life insurance is essential. If you are an important source of financial support for your family—whether or not you are married, and whether or not your baby's mother also works—you need to make sure that support continues, even if you aren't around anymore.

How much life insurance do you need? That depends on what other source of income your family will have if you die, and what other assets you have. If your life insurance policy is going to be the primary source of money for your family over a long period of time, then you should get as much life insurance as you can afford. And the best time to buy it is when you are just starting to think about having a baby.

Fortunately, life insurance doesn't have to be that expensive. Especially if you are young, healthy, and don't smoke, you should be able to obtain term life insurance at a very reasonable rate. For example, if you are in your twenties or thirties, you can get $500,000 of coverage in a twenty-year policy for only about $300 a year. That means that if you die within twenty years, then your beneficiary will get $500,000 tax-free to care for your family. You can increase your coverage to $1 million and still just pay about $500 a year.

What happens after twenty years? Ideally, by that time you will have amassed other assets that can provide for your family, or your children will be grown and able to support themselves. Or, for a few hundred dollars more each year, you may be able start off with a thirty-year policy instead.

Less well known than life insurance, disability insurance can help provide you and your family with financial support if you are injured and are no longer able to work. Because a younger father is much more likely to become disabled than to die, long-term disability insurance can be important to have. It will help to supplement any Social Security benefits that you will get, help pay your bills, and help your family to maintain their current lifestyle if you can't work anymore.

Start a College Fund for Your Baby

With all of the other things you have to worry about, thinking about how you will pay for your child's college education may be at the bottom of the list. However, the earlier you start saving, the easier it will be.

Prepaid Tuition Programs

This type of plan, often called a 529, is an education savings plan with special tax benefits. It allows you to fund one or more years of tuition now, to be used when your child is ready to start college. Unlike many other types of plans, these state prepaid tuition programs are guaranteed to pay for college in the future, even as tuition prices go up. Besides the many tax advantages, another benefit is that other family members, such as helpful grandparents, can contribute to the plan.

Prepaid tuition programs have two downsides. First, they only pay for tuition. (You will still have to save for room and board.) Second, not all states offer them. Also, for states that do offer them, the cost is likely to continue to increase each year, so paying for the plan as early as possible is a good idea.

College Savings Programs

College savings programs are another type of state 529 plan, into which you can contribute money to pay for college later. Unlike the prepaid tuition programs, there is no guarantee that the invested money will be enough to pay for all of your child's expenses. On the other hand, you can use the money for tuition, room and board, and any other college-related expenses. They also have low minimum contribution limits, which can make it easier for you to start saving for your child's college education.

Other Ways to Pay for College

Of course there are alternatives if you are unable to pay for your child's college expenses, such as loans, grants, scholarships, and other types of financial aid. Or your child may be able to work part-time as he goes to school, or he could attend a community college. Whatever your financial situation, there is always a way to get your child a college education. Long-term planning and preparation are the best ways to achieve that goal.

Just as it is never too early to begin saving for your child's college education, it is never too early to begin planning for your retirement. Most experts would say that saving for your retirement is even more important than saving for college. After all, there will be other options if you don't have enough money for your child's college expenses, but you will have fewer options when you are ready to retire.

The easiest way to set aside money for retirement is to contribute to a retirement plan at work. That is especially a good idea if your employer offers any kind of matching funds. The first step in planning for retirement is often making sure that you are contributing the maximum amount that you can to your job's retirement plan. If you aren't funding your retirement plan at work, consider cutting back on other expenses so that you can. Because you can put this money away tax-free, you are throwing away money if you don't, especially if your employer provides a matching contribution.

If your job doesn't offer a retirement plan, you may have to save on your own. An Individual Retirement Account (IRA) or a Roth IRA are good ways to do that. In addition, you can plan on your own savings and investments to help finance your retirement. If you aren't sure how to get started or are afraid to start, a financial planner can help you.

Your own retirement and your child's college education are the major investments you should begin funding as soon as possible. But they're not the only things to prepare for. Unless you're willing to live paycheck to paycheck, unprepared for any financial emergencies, there are other things that you should start saving money for.

Emergencies are one of the most important things to plan for. Besides your long-term disability insurance, do you have enough of a reserve to get by on if one or both parents can't work for a while and you miss a few paychecks? Will you be able to pay your rent or mortgage or even be able to buy groceries? If a stay-at-home parent gets sick and can't care for the kids, do you have enough money to pay for day care until the parent is better?

Saving a good three to six months' worth of your regular monthly expenses in a savings or money market account can help you be financially prepared for an emergency. Until you have that reserve or buffer built up, you should put off other unnecessary expenses, such as going on vacation or buying a new TV. Of course, you have to actually know what your monthly expenses are first, so figure out your total monthly expenditures and a regular budget and then start saving.

Consider if You Want to Have More Kids

Having more kids does introduce a lot of new expenses, including diapers, food, and perhaps increased child-care expenses. One of the highest expenses may be simply the medical cost of having another child. And of course, you will have to think about planning for more than one child to go to college. Fortunately, many other expenses are fixed, and so your total monthly expenses might not go up as much as you think as you have more kids.

For example, unless another child causes you to outgrow your home or car, your housing and transportation expenses won't increase. And you should be able to use a lot of hand-me-down clothing and baby products from your first child, so you probably won't need to buy another crib, changing table, highchair, or other baby accessories.

Once you have your emergency fund saved up and you have a plan to fund retirement and college expenses, you can begin to think about other short-term and long-term financial goals.

Your biggest goal should be to avoid any "bad" debt, such as large credit card bills with high interest rates. Paying off this type of debt, and avoiding building up more of it, is even more important than saving for college or building up an emergency fund right now.

Other goals might include buying your first house, remodeling the house you live in now, or moving into a bigger one. Other financial goals might include taking a family vacation, buying a boat, starting a business, buying a vacation home, or buying a new car. By planning in advance for some of these expenses, you can avoid building up a lot of "bad" debt and having large credit card bills that you can't pay.

Invest in Toys and Products for Your Baby

Your baby's toys might be some of the most high-tech items that you have in the house, as well as some of the most expensive. These fancy toys can talk, record your baby's voice, and even sing your baby to sleep. Some toys can be controlled by remote control, so you don't even have to go in and reset them if your baby hasn't fallen asleep yet when they stop playing.

Although not all of your toys have to run on batteries, having a few of these types of learning toys can be fun. Balls, blocks, and drums that play music, interactive dolls, and books that talk can hold your infant's attention and encourage her development.

In addition to these fun toys, you may also want to invest in some more practical products. An audio or video monitor is a great way to keep an ear or eye on your baby even when you're not in the same room with her. Another option is a combined audio and video monitor so that you can see what your baby is doing if he is crying in his room during naps or at night. It is also a good way to keep an eye on your older baby if he is playing in another room.

From a digital camera and video camcorder to record all of your baby's "firsts" to computer equipment to create movies, there are all sorts of fun toys you may want to buy for yourself as a new parent! These gadgets can be pricey, though, so don't rush out and buy anything until you do a little research.

Once you have your digital camera and video camcorder, you might consider creating a website or photo blog for your baby. This is a great way to share the joys of your baby's development with friends and family who might not be nearby. The website or blog can be as simple as a single page with a few pictures and a few lines of text that describe the picture, or a larger site with pages for each stage of your baby's development. As you get more advanced, you can add movies, stories, and even a guest book for family members to add their own comments.

Above and beyond cameras, there are other devices that high-tech dads might want to have. With all of the time that you are spending in helping to care for your baby, you will likely miss a few of your favorite TV shows. A digital video recorder, such as TiVo, can help make sure that you can still watch a few of your programs.

Other high-tech safety devices you can buy might include a wireless video camera for your backyard or a backup warning device or video camera in your car.

Part Nine: Parenting Economics

Part Ten

Looking Ahead

Congratulations! You got through the first year. It's all smooth sailing from here, right? Well, not necessarily. Each age has its own problems and challenges, so there will still be things that come up that you might be anxious about or have a hard time dealing with. Most parents do consider the first year to be the hardest, though, so you deserve a big pat on the back for making it this far.

Your baby's first birthday marks the start of the toddler years. This is the transition period between your baby's total dependency on you in his first year and his increasing independence as a preschool and school-age child. Instead of the small baby that you were bouncing on your knee, you will now have a running toddler who you will be chasing around the house.

As your child learns to walk, talk, dress, and feed himself, he will also learn to be independent in other ways. He may not want to eat when you want him to or stop playing when it is time for a nap. Or he may begin testing his limits to see what he can do and get away with. These are all normal ways that he will learn to develop and grow during this new developmental period.

Your toddler's growing mobility, independence, and need to explore will make it even more important than ever to keep his safety in mind. In addition to continuing to use a car seat in the backseat, you should inspect your house to make sure that everything is still childproofed. It is especially important that you have taken steps to childproof doors so that he can't get out of the house or into rooms that aren't safe.

During your child's toddler years, when he is running around and beginning to talk, playtime becomes more fun for many dads. It was certainly fun to play with your infant too, but now your child can really participate in play. Even when he plays alone, it is fun to watch him manipulate toys, stack blocks on top of each other, and try to figure out how things work.

In addition to simply having fun, your toddler's play-time is an important way that he learns about things. Remember that not every toy has to be computerized or have a lot of lights or sounds, though. Simple toys that he can push, pull, or climb on are just as much fun.

At this age your baby is likely to enjoy getting out more, especially once she has good head control and can sit up fairly well. You can take your baby out in a baby jogger or sports stroller, an infant carrier or sling, or just a regular stroller, to allow her to explore the world as you do things and get around too. Of course, you could simply carry her, but if you are going to be out for a while or if you are going on a long walk, a carrier or stroller will be more comfortable.

Listen for Your Baby's First Word

It's fun when your baby says his first words, especially when that word is "dada." Your baby's first word is often "dada" rather than "mama," just because it is easier to say. It is okay to feel special that his first word is "dada," but because he isn't using it as a label for either you or his mother at first anyway, you probably shouldn't attach too much significance to these first words. By about thirteen months, most toddlers are able to say "dada" and "mama" specifically to ask for or talk to their father and mother. The next word soon follows in the next few months. What will your baby's second word be? It could be "cat" or "dog," if you have either as a pet. Or maybe a sibling's name or a favorite toy, such as "ball."

The rest of your toddler's second year should lead to an explosion in his speech. By the end of the second year, many toddlers know more than fifty words and have started to talk in two-word sentences. You can also expect that he will be able to tell you a few of the things that he wants at this time. For example, he might say "milk" or "juice" when he is thirsty, or "cookie" when he wants a snack.

Even before all of this talking, your child likely will understand things very well. During his second year, he will learn to point to his body parts, such as his eyes or mouth. He will also begin to follow some two-step commands, such as "pick up the shoes, then bring them to Daddy." At the end of the second year, you can also expect him to begin pointing to things that you name, such as a toy or a cup.

140 Recognize Speech Delays

Once children start to really talk, with real words, it is easy to know when they are behind other children of the same age.

It is important to remember that just because your child isn't talking as much as other kids of the same age, it doesn't mean that she is really developmentally delayed. The range of what is considered normal is very broad. For example, one commonly used tool called the Early Language Milestone Scale-2 (ELM Scale-2) says that 25 to 90 percent of children can say four to six words between about eleven and twenty-three months. That can mean more than a full year's difference between the ages when two normal children pick up this milestone.

The range for when toddlers can say fifty or more single words is almost as broad, with most kids meeting this milestone between about eighteen and twenty-six months.

While the age range for speech development is very broad, not all speech delays are normal. You shouldn't always take a "wait and see" approach when your child isn't meeting her milestones. A toddler whose speech is delayed may have a hearing loss or other medical problem. If it also seems that your child does not understand or communicate well, she may have a more serious developmental problem that should be evaluated.

When most people think of separation anxiety, they picture a child crying as she is left at day care. For some children, even shorter separations can be difficult. Your baby may cry if you put her down, walk out of the room, or if you simply aren't paying attention to her in the same room. You can try several things to ease separation anxiety:

- Practice short separations and quickly come back to help your baby get used to it.
- Stay calm when you leave your baby and don't get overly anxious about her crying.
- Have someone distract her with a favorite toy when you leave.
- Don't leave her when she is overly tired or hungry.

Separation anxiety can be even more stressful if an infant has a strong preference for one parent and cries when that parent leaves the room. Although classically seen as happening to dads, with the baby having a preference for Mom, it usually depends on who is the primary caregiver. Either way, if you are concerned because there is a strong preference for one parent, the other parent probably needs to spend more time with the baby. And the "preferred" parent shouldn't be too quick to rescue a baby who is crying with the other parent.

Part Ten: Looking Ahead

Lessen Stranger Anxiety

Anxiety about strange people and new situations begins at about the same time as separation anxiety, and both can exist together if you try to leave your baby with a new caregiver, such as a new babysitter or new person at day care. This is a good reason not to start a new day care at this age.

More commonly, your baby will just seem a little shy or anxious when she encounters someone new while you are still with her. This may be a family member or friend who doesn't come over very often, or someone she has never met before. If you stay calm and try to slowly introduce her to these new people, she will likely get used to them too.

Remember that having separation or stranger anxiety doesn't mean that your child is spoiled or "too bonded" to his parents. Instead, it is a normal part of development and usually happens in children who have a healthy attachment to their caregivers. The lack of anxiety about strangers or separation can also be normal too.

Knowing what to give your baby to drink is one of the easier decisions that you will have to make this next year. The American Academy of Pediatrics (AAP) is very clear in recommending that kids who aren't breastfeeding should start on milk after they are a year old. If your toddler is still breastfeeding two to three times a day, he won't have to start milk until he weans down to only one feeding or stops breastfeeding altogether.

The AAP recommends that toddlers drink whole cow's milk. Younger children need some fat in their diet, and it is not recommended that you limit their fat intake until after they are two to three years old. That means no low-fat or fat-free milk until later.

The decision of what to give your toddler to drink becomes harder if he is allergic to milk. Many infants on soy formulas are able to switch to cow's milk without problems. You should still talk to your pediatrician before starting milk if your baby was intolerant of milk-based formulas. If your child only has simple formula insensitivities, and no serious allergy-type symptoms, your pediatrician might say it is okay to start milk.

Handle Milk Allergies and Other Problems

If you know your child is allergic to milk and he did well on a soy formula, you can simply continue with a soy formula, or you might change to a toddler soy formula. Soy milk is not a very good alternative, because it is low in fat.

Children who don't have milk allergies, but simply don't like milk, have many options. They can simply continue to drink a toddler formula, whether it is milk- or soy-based. Or they can just eat and drink other foods supplemented with calcium. These include cheese, yogurt, orange juice, and many other foods whose labels say that they are a "good" or "excellent" source of calcium. As a last resort, you might also consider flavoring your child's milk.

Toddlers not drinking milk are also likely to need a vitamin D supplement. In addition, you will have to be sure to make up for the fat and calories that your toddler is missing out on by not drinking milk.

About the time that infants switch to milk, most parents consider getting them to also give up their bottles. Making two big changes at the same time can be too stressful for some kids, so you might do one at a time. But which one? Should you switch to milk or to cups first?

Some parents think that it is harder to get off the bottle later if they first get their toddler used to drinking milk from a bottle. Others find it harder to get their toddler to take formula from a cup, because he has been used to drinking it from a bottle for so long.

Because there is no real right way to get your toddler used to milk and cups, you will have to think about what will work best for you. Is your toddler very easygoing and adaptable? Then you may be able to switch to both at once, using a cold-turkey approach and going straight to milk in a cup. If your toddler strongly resists any change, then consider going much more slowly. You might have to change just one bottle to milk every few days or weeks.

If your baby is breastfeeding, you can avoid bottles completely by weaning straight to a cup. Especially if your infant is already a year old when he weans, there is no real reason to give him a bottle at all. If he was drinking water or juice from a bottle, then you can switch to a cup at around twelve to fifteen months, whether or not he continues to breastfeed.

The biggest transition that comes when you go from feeding an infant to feeding a toddler isn't usually what she is eating. Sure, your toddler will be eating more "real" table food and less baby food. In fact, some kids have given up baby food altogether by the time they are a year old. The big change is usually in their eating habits.

How Much Should Your Toddler Eat?

Your older infant probably was eating three big meals each day, consisting of cereal, fruits, vegetables, and meats; three or four feedings of breastmilk or formula; and a few snacks. And that is what helped her to triple her weight that first year. All of that food and all of those calories helped fuel your infant's rapid growth. That growth slows down quite a bit in the toddler years though. Instead of gaining almost a pound a month, your toddler is expected to gain only five pounds during her whole second year. This slowdown in growth usually translates into a slowdown in eating, because your toddler needs fewer calories and less food energy now.

So instead of three big meals a day, you may find that she wants to eat only one good meal each day. She may then just pick at other mealtimes. Even if she seems picky and doesn't seem to be eating much, if she is active and growing and developing normally, then she is likely eating enough. To be sure she is eating well, review your toddler's diet with your pediatrician.

Cautions about Feeding Fish

Although fish can be a part of a healthy adult diet, there are a few reasons not to give your toddler a lot of fish to eat. For one thing, kids can be allergic to shellfish and other fish, so those foods should not be introduced to children under the age of three who are at risk for developing food allergies. The other big danger is that many types of fish are contaminated with mercury, which can harm young children, especially if they are breastfeeding and their mother eats fish.

Be careful about the types and amounts of fish that you let him eat. Specifically, younger children should not eat any shark, swordfish, king mackerel, or tilefish. Other types of fish, including shrimp, canned light tuna, salmon, pollock, and catfish, should be eaten in moderation, with no more than two servings of two to three ounces each per week.

This limit of two servings a week also applies to fish sticks and fast-food fish sandwiches. And only one of these weekly servings should be fish that you catch on your own or albacore or white tuna, which can contain higher levels of mercury. These limits and warnings also apply to the diet of women who are breastfeeding.

Prepare for Potty Training

Learning to use the potty is a big milestone for toddlers. You shouldn't expect to be able to stop buying diapers anytime soon, though. The days of trying to potty train at a very early age are mostly over—although you might still be pressured by older family members to begin potty training by nine or fifteen months.

When thinking about potty training, keep in mind that the average child doesn't begin this stage until eighteen months to three years. And most recent studies have shown that starting early, before your child is ready, usually just prolongs the whole process. This means that a child who started early would likely end up being potty trained at about the same time as children who started later.

How will you know that your child is ready? Watch for the following signs:

- Staying clean and dry for several hours at a time
- Being bothered by a dirty diaper and wanting to be changed
- Not being overly negative about things in general anymore
- Being eager to please, able to follow simple directions, and imitate others
- Having the physical ability to walk to the potty and get on and off of it by herself

It also can help if you are able to determine when your child needs to use the potty. You might already know this because she is consistent in when she goes, or because you can just tell by how she is acting. Remember that if your child isn't ready to start training, you probably should wait.

Often, the time of negativism known as the "terrible twos" starts in a toddler's second year. It is at this time that you may start noticing that your child has more temper tantrums and gets angry and frustrated when he doesn't get his way. It is important to understand that this is normal behavior. Can you really expect a toddler to understand why he can't do all of the things he wants to do, when he wants to do them? Of course not. But that *doesn't* mean that you can't work to stop these tantrums and teach him a better way to behave. Instead of giving in to tantrums (which would teach that throwing himself on the floor, banging his head, and screaming is the correct way to get things), you should try to discourage them.

The best ways to discourage tantrums are to stick with regular and predictable routines of when you do things, ignore tantrums when they occur, and try to distract your child if you see a tantrum coming. For behaviors that you can't ignore, such as hitting and biting, stay calm. A strong reaction will only encourage him to do it more.

The most important part of learning to discipline your toddler is that you should be prepared. Don't get in the habit of simply reacting to your child's behaviors, because you will be more likely to just get mad and won't be doing much to encourage better behaviors or reduce bad behaviors. You can avoid becoming the stereotypical authoritarian father by learning how to praise good behaviors, set limits, discipline in a calm and loving manner, and avoid physical punishment, such as spanking. Most important, remember that discipline is more about teaching your child how to behave. It is not all about punishment.

Throw a First Birthday Party

Like many of your baby's other firsts, the first birthday party can be a very exciting one. Your baby may or may not understand that the party is for him, but either way, the first birthday is a happy celebration for parents, friends, and other family members.

One fun trend in infant birthday parties is for your baby to have a small, separate, baby-safe cake. While you will neatly cut another cake for guests, this cake can be just for your baby, who can make a mess and simply eat it with his hands. Or maybe he will just get his face and mouth right into the cake.

These parties can be fun, even if your baby doesn't know that it's his birthday. You don't have to spend a lot of money on it by renting a Bounce House or hiring a clown. A simple, informal party can be just as much fun, especially if your baby is very shy or anxious around crowds. Try to schedule it between nap and meal times to avoid dealing with a guest of honor who is already not in the best mood because he is tired or hungry.

Early in your baby's first year, you might have doubted your decision to ever have children in the first place. After all, there were all of the sleepless nights, the hours of listening to crying, and getting spit up on all of the time. You also likely lost some freedom and the ability to be spontaneous in the things you and your partner wanted to do.

Those kinds of thoughts often quickly go away though, and they are replaced with feelings of love. That's when you realize how lucky you were to have a baby. And then you start thinking about when you are going to have another one. Should you wait one year? Two? Or more?

Is it better to space kids by several years or have them close together? There are a lot of pros and cons that support both options. Here are some factors to consider:

- Having kids close together will mean that you might have more than one infant who needs a lot of care and attention, meaning more diapers to change, more feedings, and more babies to carry around.
- Too much time between babies will mean that you will have to get used to the "baby stuff" all over again.

- An older first child might resent losing out on his only child status more if he has longer to get used to being an "only."
- Kids close in age may mean more than one or two kids in day care at the same time.
- Kids spaced far apart will have very different needs, such as an older child needing rides to school and soccer practice while the younger child needs regular naps.
- An older child might be able to entertain and help take care of younger siblings.

As you can see, there are factors that support whatever decision you make. The age at which you and your partner started having kids and how much of a support system you have will be other factors. Talk it over to come up with the situation that's best for everyone in your growing family.

Index